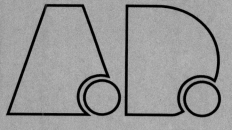

ARCHITECTURAL DESIGN

EDITORIAL OFFICES:
42 LEINSTER GARDENS, LONDON W2 3AN
TEL: 071-402 2141 FAX: 071-723 9540

EDITOR: Maggie Toy
EDITORIAL TEAM: Iona Spens, Rachel Bean,
Pip Vice, Katherine MacInnes
ART EDITOR: Andrea Bettella
CHIEF DESIGNER: Mario Bettella

CONSULTANTS: Catherine Cooke, Terry
Farrell, Kenneth Frampton, Charles Jencks,
Heinrich Klotz, Leon Krier, Robert Maxwell,
Demetri Porphyrios, Kenneth Powell, Colin
Rowe, Derek Walker

SUBSCRIPTION OFFICES:
UK: VCH PUBLISHERS (UK) LTD
8 WELLINGTON COURT, WELLINGTON STREET
CAMBRIDGE CB1 1HZ
TEL: (0223) 321111 FAX: (0223) 313321

USA AND CANADA: VCH PUBLISHERS INC
303 NW 12TH AVENUE DEERFIELD BEACH,
FLORIDA 33442-1788 USA
TEL: (305) 428-5566 / (800) 367-8249
FAX: (305) 428-8201

ALL OTHER COUNTRIES:
VCH VERLAGSGESELLSCHAFT MBH
BOSCHSTRASSE 12, POSTFACH 101161
69451 WEINHEIM
FEDERAL REPUBLIC OF GERMANY
TEL: 06201 606 148 FAX: 06201 606 184

Architectural Design is published six times per year (Jan/
Feb; Mar/Apr; May/Jun; Jul/Aug; Sept/Oct; and Nov/
Dec). Subscription rates for 1994 (incl p&p): Annual sub-
scription price: UK only £65.00, World DM 195, USA $135.00
for regular subscribers. Student rate: UK only £50.00, World
DM 156, USA$105.00 incl postage and handling charges.
Individual issues: £14.95/DM 39.50 (plus £2.30/DM 5 for
p&p, per issue ordered), US $24.95 (incl p&p).
Application to mail at second-class postage rates is
pending at Deerfield Beach, FL. Postmaster. Send ad-
dress changes to Architectural Design, 303 NW 12th
Avenue, Deerfield Beach, FL 33442-1788. Printed in
Italy. Origination by Print-Tek London. All prices are subject to change without notice. [ISSN: 0003-8504]

CONTENTS

ARCHITECTURAL DESIGN **MAGAZINE**

Battle & McCarthy • Michael Rotondi, Peter Cook Interview • Zaha Hadid • The Politics of Preservation • Books • Exhibitions

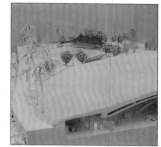

Archigram, Monte Carlo 1970

ARCHITECTURAL DESIGN **PROFILE** No 109

ARCHITECTURE OF TRANSPORTATION

Martha Rosler In the Place of the Public: Observations of a Traveller • Kenneth Powell New Directions in Railway Architecture • Cezary Bednarski Homo Itinerans • Travelling Architects • Ellerbe Becket • Nicholas Grimshaw • Renzo Piano • Richard Rogers • Shin Takamatsu • Michael Wilford • Odile Decq and Benoit Cornette • William Alsop • Gregotti Associates • Ingenhoven Overdiek Petzinka • Paul Lukez • Fentress Bradburn / BHJW

Norma Aldred, The Bartlett School, 1993

Nicholas Grimshaw & Partners, Waterloo International Terminal. Photograph Jo Reid and John Peck

GUY BATTLE AND CHRISTOPHER McCARTHY

MULTI-SOURCE SYNTHESIS
Structures Renewed Dialogue with Climatic Forces

The Gothic pioneer masons and carpenters of the 13th century developed new ways of distributing weight, dispensing with the ponderous mass of Romanesque masonry, thus assisting architecture to soar up elegantly with the penetration of daylight. By definition they were the first building engineers. Through trial and error, but with absolute confidence in their imaginations (making calculations subservient), the Gothic structural masters were able to attempt and develop audacious technical departures. In no other period has the tie between material form and natural forces been so evident.

It was a special characteristic of these first building engineers that they were also sculptors. As such, they were creative, visually confident and visually critical: their imagination and skills at work on every part of the building, developing natural forms into their structural and environmental analysis and design, and even converting a water spout into an amusing or grotesque gargoyle. In light of these observations the progress achieved by these engineers seemed to be truly miraculous. They were the real forerunners of modern high technology, replacing an equilibrium achieved by heavy masses of masonry with an equilibrium of forces created by the interplay of thrust and counter-thrust of slender ribs to be filled with light.

This engineering revolution developed into a tradition of the natural combination of gravity and climatic forces in one form; a tradition which persisted through the Gothic, Renaissance and Baroque periods until the advent of the Industrial Revolution.

It was the 'Mono Task' efficiency requirements of the Industrial Revolution which isolated structural engineering from climatic forces. This view of technology, further developed throughout the 19th and 20th centuries, is responsible for the unsatisfactorily fragmented situation of today. Valuable energy resources are expended on overcoming the climatic shortcomings of ill proportioned structures to achieve the desired internal comfort for the user of the building. However, the architectural profession has more recently gained access to advanced solar and air flow computer modelling facilities to complement the stress and strain computer software already in use. The most fascinating results may be achieved by combining this technology with the design approach of medieval master craftsmen which are yet to be experienced.

Engineering natural forces: In natural structures, forces act directly on the form, so that it is a direct response to force. In his remarkable treatise *On Growth and Form* published in 1917, D'Arcy Thompson explored the functional aspect of organic growth. He concluded that the growth of the skeletal form is to a very large extent brought about by the body's mechanical forces. His theory is illustrated by individual bones eg the hip joint, manifesting themselves as a diagram or a reflected image of the mechanical stresses explained by an idealised finite stress analysis.

Perhaps the most vivid and elementary example of forces generating form in nature occurs during the growth and movement of clouds. Clouds are ever-changing, every second of the day. As thermal effects change, cloud structure reforms to achieve equilibrium with the new forces. Natural structures and forms are evolved in a constant process of adaptation. Those systems which do not adapt, disappear. Man-made constructive growths of form, such as in structural engineering interpret the forces mathematically; the engineer must be able to assess all the forces involved, many of which may not be apparent but which act upon the structure (and indeed originate from within it). Those forces not accounted for do not disappear but remain influential, constantly demanding that the structure should change to accommodate them. For example, the penetration of solar gain and resultant overheating of a structure leads to the growth of shading in the form of overhangs and shaped columns. In the most general terms, the problem facing the engineer has always been to measure these forces and establish a method by which each force is accommodated within one form, as well as assessing the performance of the structure's response to the forces.

Interaction between natural forces, structure and materials: For a long time structural forms have been dominated by gravity. In this view the art of structural engineering has appeared to be solely associated with structural acrobatics to cope with gravity. We now understand that we live in a pluralist world where climatic molecular and atomic forces are to be incorporated within the field of structural design.

Charles Darwin suggested that survival always

OPPOSITE: Joseph Conrad L'orgueil que les navires inspirent aux hommes; The Swallow Tail rounding the Cape of Good Hope 1837. (These two images are superimposed.)

depends upon the capacity to adapt to changing circumstances. His theory holds true for structural engineering: a prediction for the future based upon a natural evolution, a reasoned and reasonable extension of ancestral trends, and the need to satisfy dynamically changing definitions of building performance and needs. Important in this strategy is the realisation that there is an established relationship between form and physical and climatic forces. It is also important that the forces are seen to exist as a series of interacting elements and are not isolated. Therefore a change in any force will naturally affect the whole.

The natural forces which a structure is to be designed for may be broken down into broad categories: gravity; interior ventilation; wind; sound; light; solar radiation; solar absorption. The natural forces can now be analysed and illustrated by a host of most advanced techniques, handed down from the masters of today's high tech industries.

Given a set of physical and climatic forces, how can we generate a single structural form which will be appropriate to all of them, and once we have established the structural form, how can we assess the aesthetic forces which arise from within it?

It is only through designing with the knowledge and feeling of a technical artist that the individual will be able to interpret the purpose of all these forces and how they may be best fulfilled within one eventual structural form.

Gravity: Perhaps the simplest device for illustrating gravitational force is by hanging like a chain a number of weights from a length of string. Structural engineers and architects alike have in the past used this analogue to generate the most appropriate geometry of a structure for a particular gravity load case.

Gaudi used the analogue of weights suspended from trees to generate the most appropriate form in stone. He constructed upside-down wire model analogues in which wires represented the columns and hanging bags of lead shot represented the eventual compressing loads. Another analogue of forces generating a form is that of a soap bubble under varying pressures and boundary conditions, the eventual form being that whereby minimum surface tension is achieved. This analogue is the principal means for 'form finding' air supported structures.

The anticlastic surfaces of tent structures are inherently 'voluminous' and 'multidirectional'. The contours of stress distribution were originally demonstrated with the use of nylon stockings, but now they may be illustrated with the visual aids of computer analysis.

A theorem by AGM Michelle made it possible to generate the cantilever form of the least-weight structure uniquely from a specification of the form. The theorem shows that all the members of

the least-weight structure must lie on one of the two families of orthogonal curves, the compression curve on one curve, and the tension on the other. The finite element analytical three-dimensional computer analysis now available provides an effective structural laboratory where one may add and subtract materials from a structural form at will until all the materials are working at the ultimate capacity, and thus achieve the required strength and stiffness for the least amount of material.

Wind forces: As structures become taller and lighter, wind load design becomes a more significant factor for the design of structures than gravity. Not surprisingly the Eiffel Tower grows from the ground as a giant multidirectional cantilever. With the need for taller chimneys, intensive research into dynamic wind flows around objects was intensified with the aid of aeronautical wind tunnel tests. Today, high-rise buildings are as common in wind tunnel test facilities as racing cars and aeroplanes.

The study of wind performance around structures goes beyond the need to predict wind dynamic forces on the proposed structure. It has led to a better understanding of wind pressures around the building for the comfort of pedestrians at ground level.

Andrew Wright of Richard Rogers Partnership has used the structural form to accelerate the wind between building block and the service core, where wind turbines are positioned to generate power for an energy self sufficient office block. A similar principle is presently being pursued by Kohn Pederson Fox for the Redevelopment of the Martini Tower in Brussels.

Wind towers have been used for ventilation for the last 3000 years, as is evident in natural construction such as termite hills. Dr Ken Yeang is presently leading research and development on ventilating high rise towers with minor wind scopes. Traditionally the understanding of wind around an object was demonstrated with wind tunnel tests. More recently, wind computer modelling is providing more realistic simulation. These design tools will pioneer new departures in architectural form from the shapes of tower blocks to the emergence of wind tower and roof scope incorporating wind power generators.

Micro convection forces: The reason for internal air flow is due to natural convection currents caused by differential temperature or because of different air pressures at different openings to the outside. These forces may be modelled by computer fluid dynamic software or by physical thermal salt model tests used to predict thermal differentials and air movement. This analysis and testing is particularly important for assessing not

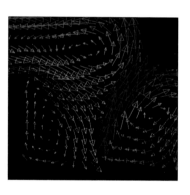

FROM ABOVE: Marseilles, 1994. *Photograph: William Alsop; computer simulation of light; computer simulation of thermal air flow; OPPOSITE: Heaven and Earth 1992, Video installation detail, 1993/94 Whitechapel Gallery Exhibition. Photograph: Kira Perov*

only ventilation flow but also fire and smoke spread to achieve safer buildings. These techniques were utilised by Willem Neutelings during the design development of the ABN-AMRO Bank Headquarters Building Proposal for Amsterdam.

Sound: The periodic motion of molecules is a form of energy called sound. If two objects are brought into contact, then some of the more intense motion of one object will be transferred to the other object. The molecules must be close to each other in order to collide. Since in air the molecules are far apart, air is not a good conductor of sound, compared to water or solid objects, and a vacuum allows no conduction of sound at all. Sound is generated through the air, and interacts with the surface of structural materials in a number of different ways: transmittance; absorption; reflection. The type of interaction that will occur is not only a function of materials but also the wavelength and frequency of the sound. The passage or sound may be analysed with the aid of computer simulation or physical sound model tests. Nick Thompson and Ljiljana Blagojevic of RHWL collaborated closely with Arup acoustics in sculpting the auditorium 'bowl' and roof to generate the final structural form of the Manchester concert hall which is presently under construction.

Force of light: The form of a structure is known to us primarily by the way it reflects light. Sensitive designs have always take into account that what we see is a consequence of how the light falls on the structure. Computer simulation generates light controls which vary as window positions alter and the angle of reflection changes. Computer modelling generates a three-dimensional interpretation of the sea of light which may be sculpted by external condition until the desired effect is achieved. Richard Jobson of Plincke Leaman & Browning has developed the form of each building of the D' Hautree School Project in Jersey in response to the daylight requirements of each specific function contained within. The classroom roofs, for example are modelled to distribute *even* daylight throughout the space, which avoids the situation where lights are switched on due to variation of light levels.

Force of solar radiation: For part of the year the sun is our friend and for part of the year it is our enemy. People used to worship the sun as a god because they understood how much life depended on it.

The sun is a huge 25M °C fusion reactor in which light atoms are fused into heavy atoms and in the process energy is released. The amount and composition of radiation reaching the earth's surface depends upon the angle which it strikes and the composition of our atmosphere.

The transmission of radiation is affected by the nature of the materials with which it interacts. Some materials are transparent to infra-red,

others absorb it and others are opaque to it. The objective of shading devices is either to reflect radiation or to absorb it and re-radiate away from the structure. To simulate shade, shadows and solar penetration, structural forms may be placed within a heliodon. This apparatus is used to simulate the shadow created by the structure at a particular point on the earth's surface, at any time of year.

Evolution of shading device: 'The solar control device has to be on the outside of the building, an element of the facade, an element of architecture. And because this device is so important as part of our architecture, it may develop into as characteristic form as the doric column.' Marcel Breuer.

Once the maximum and minimum solar angles onto the facade are determined, together with a specification for the reflection and penetration of solar radiation throughout the seasons, the types of solar shading devices may be examined in a trial and error process, including: fixed horizontal shades; fixed vertical screens; movable horizontal louvres; movable vertical blinds or fins.

In an effort to protect the external shades from the extreme effects of the climate a second glazed facade may be erected. This generates a solar updraught. This may then be used to draw air from the building, and thus aid cross ventilation, especially for high rise buildings. This is demonstrated in the proposed GSW Headquarters Building by Sauerbruch and Hutton, for which thermal analysis computer programmes (CFD) were used to simulate the thermal flue in action and show the thermal temperature variation.

Thermal mass: Heavyweight structures feel cool on hot summer days because they act as a thermal store. At night, they give up their heat by convection to the cool night air and by radiation to the cold outer atmosphere at absolute zero – thus 'recharging' their heat sink capability for the next day.

David Emond of RH Partnership has developed the Ionica Headquarters Building which maximises the thermal mass of the concrete slabs, with the passage of air supply through the hollow cores of standard precast concrete floor slabs to provide a source of free summer cooling during mid season and summer periods.

Thermal resistance: The opposition of materials to the flow of heat by conduction, convection and radiation is called thermal resistance measured largely as a function of the number and size of air spaces that they contain. This is commonly known as the insulative properties of materials. The high performance insulative materials developed for space suits have insulative properties equivalent to meters of concrete. However, under hot and cold dynamic conditions, 120mm of concrete may

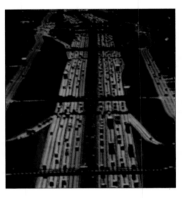

FROM ABOVE: Simultaneous response by shoal of hatchet fish; Los Angeles Freeway, 1994; Maurice Brennan Energies in Ebullition

appear to have a greater resistance than 10mm of timber. This is due to the time lag of the concrete mass heating up. The 'insulating' effects of mass is most beneficial in hot dry climates during the summer. This effect is not helpful in humid climates where the temperature remains constant.

Interpretation of climatic forces: Paul Cézanne, reacted against the lack of structure in the work of the impressionists and declared his intention to make impressionism into 'something solid and durable'. Cézanne's rigorous analysis of structure has made him one of the fathers of modern art, an inspiration to abstract artists through his painstaking analysis of colour which replaced light and shade as his means of modelling.

It is fascinating studying an artist at work. One may observe the whirl of the brush in a flashing stroke across the canvas or the gouging of the clay to form beautiful works of art. Whether or not the final result of such energy is recognisable image, it is the process itself which becomes a work of art – unlike traditional artists of the pre-twentieth century. Such contemporary artists are not preoccupied with a pictorial physical image but by balance of sensations and images: motion/stability, strength/weakness, tension/strain, light/dark, hot/cold, noise/silence; indeed, the main ingredients of engineering. There is a mystical quality in abstract art which is difficult to explain but so true to interpretations of natural forces.

Duithuit, in the catalogue of an exhibition of paintings by Riopelle in 1945, wrote of 'the work of this French-Canadian painter – a kind of aerial impressionism, extremely fickle, adapting its own fury to the capacity of the executor, and the ruling of its own in powerful rhythms. Most painters desire to be a force of nature integrated into nature and to lose control in order to gain a certain explosive vigour, a constant source of masterpieces'. Similarly this energising can be applied to an interpretation of natural forces effecting in architecture. We should first channel our understanding of the interaction of structural form with physical and climatic forces on paper as force and flow diagrams expressing technical performance.

There are many ways of expressing the interaction of structural materials and form with physical and climatic forces in all the surging seas of contemporary searching towards meaningful diagrammatic expression. When collaborating with the architect Will Alsop on the Marseilles Hotel du Départment, although part of Ove Arup Partnership we did not necessarily 'see' environmental performance of the structure completely in our minds before beginning to sketch environ-

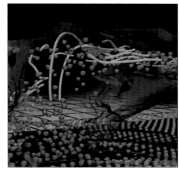

mental force diagrams or to model structural form with Will Alsop; nor was an image conceived of a structured environment which had only to be sketched on paper with a pencil, or visualised electrical technics. Generally, a sense of Alsop's intentions was the starting point, with the environment illustrated by a series of paintings, but it was not possible to define clearly and predict a conclusion without proceeding with a degree of analytical trial and error.

The engineer's perception of structural form and orientation, and the image of environmental performance, grows with the architect's vision; from the first pencil stroke on the paper to the last in an organised manner, one touch demanding another. Sketching an image of the predicted environmental performance of a structure is in some ways an act of three-dimensional elimination, in that one sets up a structural model, a column here and an exposed slab overhang there, making adjustments and correcting relationships as one works to eliminate and sketch over irritations of poor daylight penetration, lack of thermal mass, lack of cross-ventilation due to faulty composition and indecisive structural form and materials, until the image of an environmentally efficient structural form seems complete and whole.

We are, at this moment in the world's history, part of a privileged elite with an unparalleled opportunity to develop renewed interpretations of natural forces associated with building physics. There are thousands of climatic and atmospheric laboratories and computer analytical programmes which are readily available to be explored with universities, and consultants are dedicated to analysing and testing physical and climatic performance with form and ready to communicate this. The similar minded scientists and artists should be encouraged to participate in the realisation of architecture's image in collaborative efforts to create form from formless matter of mutual physical and climatic stimulation in the spirit of cooperation in coordinating differences. One can only imagine what Gaudi would have created beyond the hanging chain analysis if computational physical and climatic computer and laboratory facilities of today were made available as he was modelling the Guell Chapel in Barcelona.

The authors wish to acknowledge the contribution made by Maurice Brennan to this article.

FROM ABOVE: Computer simulation of air movement inside a cloud; The Capsizing of Garthsnaid *September 1911; vapour trails after high speed particle collision*

MICHAEL ROTONDI, PETER COOK
AN ARCHITECTURAL DESIGN INTERVIEW

*T*he pluralistic condition that exists in
architecture at the moment means that a
reassessment of architectural education,
*from which such plurality stems, is not only timely
but essential. It is a subject which should be
central, not only to pupils and educators but to
the profession as a whole, since these students
are the architects of the future and must be
adequately equipped to take responsibilty for its
buildings. To do this, they now need a multi-
faceted education which allows them to develop
not only the essential design flair, but also public
relations skills, organisational patterns and
managerial ability. Two key educators from either
side of the Atlantic – Peter Cook from the Bartlett
in London and Michael Rotondi from SCI- Arch in
Los Angeles – have combined forces in order to
provide one of the most progressive educational
formulae in architecture today. Together with
Maggie Toy of* Architectural Design *they discuss
their hopes and aims to reassess the effective-
ness of our schools of architecture worldwide.
Maggie Toy began this discussion by asking
Michael Rotondi what he thought of the state of
architectural education at this time.*

Michael Rotondi: On the one hand I think it's
probably at its peak but I also think that it's time
that radical changes start to happen. The decen-
tralisation of power and authority that's occurring
in society and politics has to somehow find it's
way into the educational system. The old paradigm of the master-disciple is no longer workable
both for philosophical and practical reasons.
Students now have a lot more information available to them through electronic media and the
simultaneous correlations that they can make in
processing this information are a lot more sophisticated and advanced than the people that are
teaching them. The basis for the canon for
architectural education is no longer workable.

MT: Is architectural education too wide – particularly in the States where those from all angles of
education can join classes on architecturally
based subjects? Should it be split into, for want of
a better definition, theorists and practitioners to
accommodate the range from philosophical
theory classes to those classes in which you are
up to your elbows in plaster?

MR: Education isn't too wide. I think it's too
narrow in its practice in terms of how people
practise within the different subcultures in architecture. We have to learn how to integrate more
ideas more effectively. Seven years ago we
calculated that the number of classes that the
students had to take from the time they entered till
the time that they graduated had increased
eightfold. In the 50s the education system pre-
supposed that an architect was a generalist in
terms of his or her intelligence, but had very
specific skills in terms of the application of that
intelligence. Students today are taking five
different classes every semester, and they do that
two semesters a year, for anywhere from three to
five years which means that there is very little time
for them to integrate all of that information into a
body of knowledge. We realised that we couldn't
eliminate a lot of the subject matter but we began
to make it easier by integrating it into larger
wholes so that the students could begin to see the
relationship between activities, thoughts and
actions so that everything that they did had a
common cause. From that period seven years
ago we encouraged the students to identify
themselves not so much as architects but as
people interested in bigger ideas that they just
happen to explore through the medium of architecture. Ultimately, those ideas are manifest in
form, which we call architecture.

Peter Cook: I think the really interesting thing is
that the 'cutting edge' practitioners are actually
alchemists too. There are many situations where
the kind of thinking that's going on is exploring
ways of being more viable, investigating a combination of apparatus, criteria, methods or experiences – that borrows quite graciously from every
part of creativity. I think that comes from very
large 'studio' or 'experimental' offices and the
problem is going to be with the middle offices –
those motivated to give their local audience what
it is familiar with. So you could say, if you were
extremely cynical, that there would be certain
schools for the offices which would really be
going into the 21st century and other schools that
would be turning people back to the 19th century.

MT: How do you go about creating an atmosphere or level of inspiration amongst the young
architects within your school?

MR: The way we've done it is by serving up role models. Creative people look at the world in three ways: analytically, critically and then they operate in a generative way. We find people that function in that way, who are continually looking forward while they move forward, and who are as curious and as fearless now as they were when they were children, but with a high degree of skill and wisdom. We bring in people who are inspired and who work in an inspired way and are interested in nurturing the students as opposed to controlling them. They tend to give the students the same privilege that they want to be given themselves, which is to be able to propose ideas and to explore those ideas in ways that make them feel comfortable at taking risks and making mistakes. Inspiration – to inspire is to breathe into. Teaching is very much like inhaling and exhaling which is a very simple but profound process of the human body. We used to think that education was primarily putting into and not letting anything come out in its natural form, we wanted it back out in the way that it was put in, but this is just reconstitution as opposed to invention. This independent search for the truth is what SCI-Arc was founded on and it's pretty much the way that it continues to this day.

MT: How did the collaboration between your schools begin?

MR: The collaboration started between Peter and myself though it's really between Peter and the world. Peter is in my mind probably the equivalent of the Secretary General of Architecture. He's the ambassador for architecture to the world and like a bee, pollinates all of the flowers in his peripatetic travelling and through his insatiable curiousity to continually find things that haven't been found yet , and then shares all of his findings with everyone else. This is the basis for anybody's collaboration with Peter, but we started bringing Peter to the school since it started 20 years ago. I brought him here, from the beginning of my tenure as director, to invigorate the school and he brought students with him, who made friends with our students, who in turn wanted to go and visit them.

PC: Yes, I think it's basically a historical thing, this English love affair with Los Angeles. The whole archetype group were very involved with Los Angeles at the end of the 1960s. In the last number of years since Michael's been running SCI-Arc he has changed it for something with a much stronger intellectual base. My case is quite different, which is that I came from a creative base to a fusty institution which had existed for 100 years. So he's got what I would call in broad terms a much tougher and wittier intellectual

atmosphere in contrast to what was already a potentially creative or had a tradition of being – so it's the reverse tactic. I think it's that he and I trust each other. Incidentally, I hope that the traffic will be slightly more two way now rather than the guys from London appearing in Los Angeles. I would like the north end of Bloomsbury to be as familiar territory with not only Michael but his colleagues or faculty or anybody dropping by.

MT: How do your students benefit from the collaboration?

MR: I think seeing the world and how things are done in other places, how people live in other places, and how architecture is done in other places. It literally and figuratively broadens their horizons by being able to move around the world. Our aim for all of the exchange programs that we've set up in the last seven years is to prevent students from developing a provincial outlook by encouraging them to travel all over the world. In doing that they're not only making friends, but they're learning first hand about the history of architecture and a theory begins to develop out of that. They develop a broader understanding of architecture and because European culture is so much more developed than our own they are able to broaden the context within which architecture can be understood and practised.

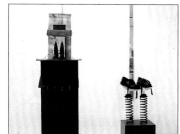

PC: I think that there are several exchange systems going in Europe at the moment like Erasmus and so on. There are all sorts of students moving between schools. They are usually people who move for the sake of it without any serious follow up. I think the really dynamic aspect of this collaboration derives from the fact that both schools see themselves as experimental and both schools, I suppose, are in interesting cities and therefore when you move between the two places you're not *just* moving. I think the point that Michael made about the faculty members is very important because it's not just a question of eagle-eyed young students arriving from another city but it's also when the discussions get, dare I say it, 'professional'. They get to be created in terms of cause and effect – the idea of the 'ongoing seminar'. I think the really intriguing thing about it is our reciprocal arrangement with SCI-Arc is that it is the ideal condition for school which is almost answerable to no one apart from the acquisition board. I think that it connects with the philosophical condition that Michael's talking about, but it's also the continuing of the traditional home of the creative eccentric.

MT: Does the location of the schools assist or hinder the collaboration? I imagine the 'learning

SCI-Arc School: student work

atmospheres' in each city are quite different.

MR: Yes, they are, but I think that's a plus. However, the learning atmosphere at the Bartlett and at SCI-Arc has a lot in common. SCI-Arc, when it was founded was inspired by the English scene as it was embodied in the AA, and ever since then I think a lot of things that we've done here, whenever we've made major decisions in the past, we often thought how would our friends at the AA make these same decisions? I think that in spirit the two schools are very similar but the bureaucratic structures that are part of the institutional structures in each country are very different. The only difference, I think, is ultimately that all of our creative energy goes into the work and not into the bureaucratic and institutional structures. I think that historically in England a lot of energy goes into work as well, but a lot of energy there comes from having that resistance put up to them, and probably we can learn from that also.

PC: I always felt that narrowness of the sort of standard part of architecture which was always reinforcing rule systems. My God it's a bag of institutionalised resistances whether it's in order to preserve architecture or the word or the idea of building or the idea of society as we used to know it, etc, etc. I think university departments around the world are reinforcing this preserve, although some of them have weirdos in cupboards. I think our responsibility is to bring them out of the cupboards and to encourage the alchemy. I don't begin to understand all the methods that some of my younger friends use. I see people playing with some weird thing on the end of a line somehow. Not only is everyone talking about virtual reality, including some of the reactionaries, but they'll mouth virtual reality at you as if they would have mouthed Venturi a few years ago! The real thing is alchemy, but the key to architectural education is having what I call having the 'wizards' around or the 'Pied Pipers' – I don't quite know what sort of an analogy to give it.

MT: Have either of you implemented anything you have seen in the other school into your own?

MR: From the founding of SCI-Arc we've implemented a lot of things that we interpret as having been done at a lot of places, in particular at the AA where most of the significant architects have taught and practised, from the late 60's up until the present. We'll find and use good ideas from any source. If SCI-Arc was a bird it would be the magpie.

MT: Peter, have you any plans for improvement at the Bartlett, do you think you need change or are you satisfied with the status quo?

PC: We are still climbing at the moment. The thing to watch is when people with very probing positions become comfortable with each other and do a sort of over-to-you-Charles kind of thing in a debate or in an assessment or whatever. When you get around 400 souls there are subdynamics. What I would like to hear is not from somebody, 'Oh, that's what that school does'. You'll get different stories depending on which gang of people you talk to and the relationships are always changing between the different groups of people. It is not a stylistic thing, it's more to do with the sorts of conversations people are having – like this year there are tremendous numbers of different groups talking about basing projects on the fetishes or idiosyncrasies or hobbies or collecting manias of individual students. We've noticed it has shifted to slightly less people doing hands-on model building and more people collecting things. If you want to be really dynamic I don't think you necessarily have to have a giant revolution in the school – a dynamic institution should adapt to these developments. If you go back a four year period it has completely turned itself around, and I think that happens when a school is very healthy.

MT: Do you think that the fact that you are both known as practising architects assists your educational skills?

MR: It definitely assists our skills in that whatever it is that we're proposing, we've probably tested in some form in practice. I think it also gives some credibility in what we do and say to the students as well as in terms of what reputations the schools have around the world. I think that probably most important is that here at SCI-Arc we've never seen the separation between theory and practice and we've constantly worked to merge educational practice and professional practice. When you begin to see architectural practice as a generative activity that is based on having a critical eye and a keen mind, I think it's essential that both of those practices are integrated and not kept apart. We're trying to bring people in at a formative age, and put them through a number of experiences that are going to help enlighten them as well as helping them to develop skills that will ultimately allow them to go out in the world and build some things that make a difference.

PC: The danger in the British situation is that the idea of the practising teacher is not being encouraged. We have schools which have a high proportion of practising teachers – you have to fight for this against the system. We have career teachers on some sort of salary scale and grading system

ABOVE: Adrian Friend, Zoologischer Garten; BELOW: Andy MacFee, Berlin project. (Bartlett School)

and then say: well there must be a connection with the architectural profession. That is very much peculiar to this country – it's almost certifiable in other parts of Europe.

MT: How does the experience of running a practice affect the way you approach the role of running a school?

MR: An institution that is like ours operates somewhere between complete anarchy and complete totalitarianism. We're really exploring, in a variety of forms, the relationship between structure and freedom, and the role that one plays as a leader of an institution like this varies from time to time, from moment to moment. Sometimes you run it with a heavy hand and at other times you run it as if you're a ghost floating through the halls. And I think most of the time now I see it especially as someone who is trying to give some direction to a self-organising system, which sounds like a *non-sequitur*. SCI-Arc has continues to be very much like an organism that somehow develops in mysterious ways and takes form that comes from the energy field that is a result of everyone who is here as opposed to one person. The only thing that I can do to influence the direction of the school is in my choice of the people who come here. After they arrive – and the overall idea of the place is discussed along with some possibilities for the direction that specific areas of the school can go in, and what the relationship is in my mind between all of the different parts of the school to each of the people that are in leadership positions – then they're pretty much left alone to do whatever it is that they do best. Periodically we then talk about what is going on in order to self-correct.

MT: Peter, what do you see your role in school – is it the same as Michael's?

PC: I think in some respects we are very similar. There are some extraordinary teachers who can get fantastic results. Their alchemy level is quite high and in a way they're often rather childlike, once the seance is broken, they're left kind of blinking. However I suppose, by being 'captain of the ship', you want there to be different kinds of psychological games going on. One is always intrigued to follow the path of these different psychologies. The late Alvin Byarsky could engage the creative enthusiasm in somebody at a certain moment, not too early, not too late and get them involved through trickery or some other methods. There are one or two places which have

interesting people running them – Tschumi in Columbia . . . Hejduk is something special again. John is such a guru and is so mystic, but there is certainly an aura about that school. It's almost that it should be kept in a special preserve – it's much more special than either of our two schools in the sense that our doors are constantly open and the windows slightly rattling – almost like church in many respects.

MT: So you have probably taken some measures from Alvin Byarsky – is that what you're saying?

PC: Well I just mentioned in passing that I think it would be inaccurate not to. I think schools are as good as the people in them at a particular time.

MT: Have you taken anything from Michael's school on the visits that you've made there?

PC: I think Michael's school also reads the whole psychology of the way in which LA is an incredibly multi-stranded and creative place where mythology becomes reality more easily than it does in Europe where we have, as soon as somebody suggests that a bit of mythology becomes reality, someone who comes up and suggests that it already has – or that it can't.

MT: The collaboration requires a large amount of entrepreneurial skill – does this initiative come solely from the two of you?

MR: In order to be good in anything, to have highly developed sensibilities and intelligence and then use those effectively in the world, you have to have entrepreneurial skills. I think in the most obvious ways it did come solely from the two of us, but then we're also responding to the energy at our backs, and all of the people that want this type of collaboration to occur. What we're doing is just creating the conditions for our students and faculty to spend time together, both in Los Angeles and in London. What Peter's skill has really been, I think, is in trying to show everybody what they have in common rather than what their differences are. I think Peter sees the world as one place and considers the architectural community to be part of the world and to be one place. In this exchange programme I think that not only do the students and faculty have a lot to learn from each other, but that Peter and I have much to learn from each other also.

ABOVE: Carolyn Butterworth Cushion; *BELOW: Adrian Bower* Fire *(Bartlett School)*

ZAHA HADID
VITRA FIRE STATION
Weil am Rhein, Germany

The Vitra Fire Station was developed, not as an isolated object, but as the outer edge of the landscaped zone, defining space rather than occupying space. At her recent RIBA lecture, Zaha Hadid showed how the project developed through numerous studies: drawings, models, paintings showing light, mass, landscape and movement. The sketches focused on the fusion of architecture and context – showing the surrounding landscape streaming into the building. The dynamic walls alternate between void and volume allowing the building to be at once secure and enclosing while giving the impression of imminent speed and escape.

The geometry of the building derives from and expresses the crossing of the two main organising geometries of this area: the collision of directions between the agricultural complex and the large field of railways is reflected in the fire station. The architectural concept has been developed into a linear, layered series of walls. The programme of the fire station inhabits the spaces between these walls which puncture, tilt and break according to the functional requirements. As one passes across the spaces of the fire station, one catches glimpses of the large red fire engines. Their lines of movement are inscribed into the ground; a series of choreographic notations. The whole building is movement, frozen. It expresses the tension of being on the alert and the potential to explode into action at any moment.

The walls appear to slide past each other, while the large sliding doors literally form a moving wall. The design unifies two very different parts of the programme; the housing of firetrucks, and the provision of various facilities for the fire-fighters. The concept of the stacked walls encompasses both parts, whereby the intersection of the two is expressed by a break or bend in the line of the building. The entrance to the building is precisely at this junction.

The whole building is constructed of exposed, reinforced *in-situ* concrete. This proved to be the most suitable medium with which to realise sculptural expressiveness and structurally ambitious long spans and cantilevers. Special attention was given to the sharpness of all edges, any attachments like roof edgings or claddings were avoided, as they detract the simplicity of the prismatic form and the abstract quality of the architectural concept. This same absence of detail informed the frameless glazing, the large sliding planes enclosing the garage and the treatment of the interior spaces.

The interiors of those spaces that require insulation are rendered. The sanitary wall is tiled in glass mosaic. The lockers which mediate between the changing and fitness areas are made from steel and stainless steel respectively. A golden wall tilts outwards at the end of the fitness room.

The lighting is integrated into the architecture and is based on the concept of lines, rather than points. These lines are set into the planes as cuts from which light emanates, rather than as bodies which obtrude into the space. The lines of light direct the necessarily precise and fast movement through the buildings.

The Fire Station bears testament to Hadid's reputation as an assertive, sculptural architect and to her unique ability to transcend building mass with pure anti-gravitational sensual energy.

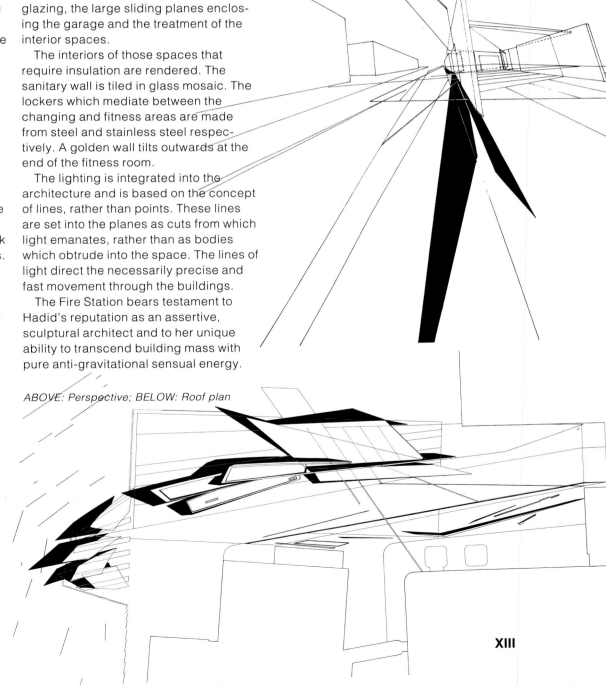

ABOVE: Perspective; BELOW: Roof plan

THE POLITICS OF PRESERVATION

Preservation, or 'listing', is popularly thought to be a benign process through which a building can be protected 'in aspic' for an indefinite period of time. However Peter Brooke, Secretary of State for Heritage, explains that listing 'creates a presumption in favour of a building's preservation but it does not necessarily mean that a building must be preserved whatever the cost; its main purpose is to ensure that care is taken over decisions affecting its future'. This academic, dry and legalistic approach belies the passion that decisions surrounding listing arouse. The process of listing involves someone choosing what they think is, or will be, of historic interest. Inevitably this provokes an outcry from those who disagree with the choice, the ideas that that building stands for and the amount that it will cost in upkeep. Far from being a straightforward procedure, listing or preservation is a focal point of interaction between politics, ideas and art – who decides which buildings should be preserved and who then decides whether to allocate necessary funding. Betraying his own sympathies, Peter Moro said in an interview with Kenneth Powell '[Margaret] Thatcher slashed public spending . . . and in due course the Prince of Wales derided modern architects . . . a bad combination'.

The general rule is that a building should be over a certain age before it is listed to prevent this problem of the inclusion of properties only associated with contemporary values. Some argue that if a building is worth protecting, it should be protected while still intact in order to ensure proper maintenance and prevent the need for extensive restoration. However, the British adhere to the 30 year rule, the USA to a 50 year time lapse and in Australia the Burra Charter has no official time limit but the average 'cut off' is 1960.

Partly due to the fact that the required time is up and partly for defensive reasons to prevent demolition, there has been an international surge of interest in a programme to preserve post 1945 architecture recently. More than the preservation of any other era, postwar architecture reveals the public, historical and political arguments which surround any decisions made concerning preservation. Paul Finch acknowledges that there has been '(legitimate) public criticism of poor quality postwar housing and office design'. Though much of this architecture has not been universally liked, historians argue that the ideas that it represents make it an essential part of the historic fabric of our time. One of the unique aspects of postwar architecture concerns the aim for a factory made building turned out by industrial production techniques in an attempt to increase productivity after the war. The aircraft and vehicle production industries had a considerable influence on the ideas of architects and structural engineers. New building types emerged: light prefabrication, commercial 'roadside' development, large retail spaces 'chain stores' and multi-storey blocks of flats.

After a muddled start six years ago, in 1992 English Heritage embarked on a three-year research programme into the main postwar building types. The United States National Register has planned a conference for early next year to discuss 'Preserving the Recent Past'. The Australian Heritage Commission has commissioned the Royal Australian Institute of Architects to undertake a study of significant 20th-century buildings in each state.

Unlike restoration of traditional buildings, the preservation of modern buildings has to be approached from two angles – type and technique. The problem of fragility or short life span of particular 'types' of properties is addressed by Beth Savage of the Washington based National Register. In her article 'Disappearing Ducks and Other Recent Relics' The Journal of Preservation Technology, Beth Savage blames factors such as 'changing economic or social conditions, the ephemeral or obsolete nature of building materials or the processes by which they were manufactured or environmental effects . . . accelerated rate of change, planned obsolescence and "progress"'. The National Register has already taken steps to preserve retail and entertainment properties and prefabricated suburban housing. It has listed a 1950s porcelain enamelled steel Lustron House in Chesterton, Indiana, which was regarded at the time as the 'all metal dream house'. In Britain, the systematic development of various methods of prefabricated schools such as Greenfield, Hertfordshire indirectly contributed towards free education. Limbrick Wood Infant School, Coventry was built using aluminium at a time when aircraft industries were being run down. Limbrick Wood and Woodlands, a steel prefabricated secondary school, were built by the

Ministry of Education as prototypes. Though these structures were designed to be finite, Elaine Harward of English Heritage suggests that their inherent adaptability means that their extended life is, in fact, feasible. The main problem with such buildings is insulation which was not considered to be such a high priority in the 1950s when fuel was relatively cheap.

From a different angle, Robert Thorne of Alan Baxter & Associates argues that the revolutionary change in building form after the war means that a building is conceived as a perfectly finished object. This change in 'type' means that patch repairs used on traditional buildings will have to be replaced by more extensive renewal or fac-simile replacement in order to maintain the integrity of the whole.

Technically, the use of new materials from reinforced concrete to aluminium and plastics, and new techniques such as new jointing sys-tems, and new combinations of structure and finish, pose new problems. The extensive use of reinforced concrete suffered not only from rusting of the metal reinforcement but from concrete spalling where a condition known as 'concrete cancer' or 'alkaline aggregate reaction' causes the concrete to weaken and come away from the reinforcement.

Some materials and techniques that were used have not survived the test of time and may require much more maintenance than traditional tech-niques and building fabrics. However 'traditional' buildings also demand expensive maintenance in the sense that the skills needed to replace a cornice on, for example, an 'Adam building' are scarce and expensive – there is still no such thing as a 'maintenance free product'.

The new level of maintenance required by prefabricated, commercial and high rise architec-ture that characterises the postwar era forces us to reassess the fundamental question of why we list buildings. Do we want to preserve these buildings because of the psychological impact of the built environment, for historical reasons – 'posterity', architectural interest etc? The main question is whether the cost of maintaining or restoring some modern buildings outweighs their historical value. Robert Thorne asks 'Are they to be regarded as a separate category, in which demolition is more permissible because extensive repairs are so costly? Or will the conservation authorities adopt them as a special cause, meriting a large slice of the conservation budget? Will it have to be decided that the legacy of the postwar period will be represented by a very few fully conserved examples, a much tighter selec-tion than for any previous period?'

Alternatively, should we just document these buildings and take photographs rather than pouring money into their restoration and mainte-nance? Dennis Sharp, Chairman of DOCOMOMO-

UK (Documentation and Conservation of Buildings, Sites and Neighbourhoods of the Modern Movement) insists that we should step up efforts to set up a modern architecture archive. He claims that Paris, Amsterdam, Helsinki, Brussels and other EC cities have set up archives and museums that provide working study centres on the architecture of this century and promote and develop exhibi-tion and publishing programmes and that Britain must not be left behind.

This solution is fraught with controversy: once the building is removed the photogra-phers word becomes gospel. Should we document all the stages of the building or just the original design before alterations? Is it realistic to assume that people would actively look up this information anyway? Over 30 thousand people visit Blenheim Palace, Oxfordshire, England, every year; but how many of these would know about it if it had been razed to the ground (as its contemporary Whig critics would have liked) and they had to visit a library for information? This is a political example but to take a more recent example based on the issue of maintenance costs – how would it effect future generations if Frank Lloyd Wright's buildings were documented and then demolished? His ubiquitous cantilevered flat roofs leak, sag and have even fallen in and other components he favoured have frequently proved defective and hard to maintain. The cost of restoring every Wright building in the USA to perfect condition was recently estimated at $1 billion.

One of the most controversial cases of poten-tially 'financially unfeasible restoration' in Britain at the moment, concerns Keeling House, 1955-9, London, a public housing tower block built by Sir Denys Lasdun and recently listed by Peter Brooke. Brooke defended his decision thus: 'I am aware of the structural and technical problems associated with Keeling House and the various estimates of the costs of repairing it. But the legislation requires that . . . once I consider a building to have such special interest, then I may not take into account the costs of repair or the consequences of listing in other ways.'

This approach is also true of the USA and Australia. Obviously the criteria of 'historical interest' and 'funding' are distinct, firstly as a result of the time lapse required by listing organi-sations to attain an objective stance during which time the building may have deteriorated, and secondly because of the fact that listing does not protect indefinitely but encourages careful consideration concerning future treatment and funding. The financial problem of maintaining or restoring buildings is the Achilles' heel of listing. Logically listing is only as effective as the amount of funding, public or private, available. However,

ABOVE: Limbrick Wood 1951-52, Infant School, Coventry, UK (listed). Photograph: Elaine Harwood; BELOW: Lustron House 1950s, Chesterton, Indiana, USA (listed). Photograph: The Journal of Preservation Technology

who should be responsible for choosing buildings that demand extensive restoration, such as Keeling House, to be listed?

There are two distinct schools of thought here: firstly 'architectural historians know best' and secondly 'shouldn't the general public be allowed to choose whether they agree with this manner of spending public sector money?' The controversial postwar Brutalist style of architecture, manifested in the South Bank which has been the subject of an exhibition at the Architecture Foundation, illustrates the complexity of this problem. Clare Hyde at the Centre's press office claims that there are as many arguments for as against – 'take the aesthetic issue for example – while some people consider that it should be "greened" others like the monolithic, "Mayan temple" atmosphere that the raw masonry creates'.

Francis Golding of the UK branch of ICOMOS (International Council on Monuments and Sites) claims that there is evidence to suggest that architectural historian's taste is in advance of the general public. While I agree that this is often the case, Golding's assertion should be weighed against a recent event concerning multi-storey blocks of flats, one of the most representative types of postwar architecture. The 'event' in question is the demolition of 400 flats in Glasgow, designed by Sir Basil Spence. James Dunnett, a conservationist, spoke of the 'powerful rhythm of their row of linked towers' and Lord Palumbo predicted that they would come to be seen as 'seminal works of art in the context of public housing'. However the flats were damp, windy, vandalised and hopelessly unsuited to the climate. *The Independent* (13.9.93) reported that 'architectural historians lamented the demolition while local inhabitants applauded'.

The architectural historian's approach presumably excludes both extremes – not only the public, but respected practising professionals who might be motivated by self interest or be unable to be objective. Among others the Architecture Foundation exhibition showed Terry Farrell's scheme for the South Bank area which he describes as 'the anti-urban era of modernism. The [existing] scheme makes little reference to the city and its surrounding context, and merely serves to reinforce its isolated nature'. Dr Diane Kay at English Heritage claims that views have changed since Farrell's original scheme to alter the appearance of the structure and that, since the public is 'the most fickle mistress', they will change again.

Educating the public into an appreciation of modern architecture seems to be the obvious architectural historian's answer. Peter and Alison Smithson's Economist Building is listed grade one but DOCOMOMO has organised the recent retrospective of the work of the movement's main protagonists in order to encourage a public

reassessment look at the Brutalist legacy. Although Brutalism had an international impact manifested in a return to principles of austerity, honesty and material roughness, the Smithsons are more widely respected in Europe than at home.

The issue of public involvement is a fundamental problem in Japan where the architect Kisho Kurokawa claims that there is as yet no attempt to list post-1945 buildings, since the question of financial responsibility whether public or private cannot be solved. Looking to previous examples, Maki Yasumori, the manager of the Architectural Institute of Japan, confirmed that even preservation of pre 1945 listed buildings amounts to a letter from the AIJ saying 'We hope you will use your important architecture carefully' so that preservation 'depends on the owner's good will and judgement'. Kurokawa has taken the initiative and created a precedent for public funding by listing important modern assets since 1980 with financial support from the Ministry of Education.

In England, the English Heritage expenditure for 1992/93 was £115.7m of which £101.9m was provided by Central Government. Grants are awarded according to the funding available. Two examples of 1930s buildings demonstrate the level of funding that can be expected once the postwar lists go through. English Heritage provided 40% of the £420,000 plus needed to restore Mendelsohn & Chermayeff's De La Warr Pavilion at Bexhill but, while they agreed to up-grade Amyas Connell's White House, Surrey from a Grade II to a Grade II (star), they refused a grant. Restoration is not the only demand on government money and indeed the recent maverick grant of £100,000 from Wealden District Council, for the restoration of a Grade II private house in Uckfield, Sussex, has provoked outrage amongst local taxpayers.

In America, there are tax incentives for properties considered to be 'income producing' by the internal Revenue Code and tax credits on 'easements' but only a very small amount of Federal funding is available to each State preservation office and in the recession many of these sources have dried up. Beth Savage concludes that without 'more favourable economic incentives for preservation, many more significant properties of the recent past will disappear'. One new problem area is commercial property where some owners are reluctant to maintain their buildings once they seem to have become obsolete. This has prompted the appearance of the Society for Commercial Archaeology in America. The 1953 McDonald's Drive-in Restaurant in Downey, California exemplifies the problem. It was determined eligible for listing in 1984 as the earliest remaining original McDonald's

ABOVE: Peter and Alison Smithson, The Economist Building 1959-64, London (listed); BELOW: GLC Architects, South Bank Centre 1967-68, London (certificate of immunity from listing). Photograph: English Heritage

hamburger stand in the country but its fate is now in question since the McDonald's corporation announced that they were closing the restaurant because 'it is too small to modernise and is losing money'.

Lord Gowrie's advice might follow along the lines of his outrageous statement in *Building Design* (21.1.94) – 'If a building becomes redundant for the business it was originally built for it should be knocked down and replaced'. While Francis Golding claims that the architectural profession does not on the whole take these decisions, it inevitably effects them, relieving architects of any responsibility to the public, the economy and the environment.

A less outrageous solution might be adaptation. William McKee, Director of the British Property Federation admires the principle of listing as long as those responsible are sensitive to adaptation. Wimbledon Town Hall, London built in the 1930s became part of a new shopping development. English Heritage was initially against increasing the size of the entrance way which was too small for its new role but were ultimately persuaded that the alteration was necessary. Should potential adaptability be central to English Heritage's selection criteria? Dr Diane Kay claims that with 3,000 cases per year it would be a mistake to waste time and effort assessing the economic viability of each building.

Adaptable buildings can be rented and the returns on this rent constitute an attractive investment. In 1991, English Heritage approached the Royal Institution of Chartered Surveyors to explore perceptions of historic buildings in the commercial property market and particularly to discover how listed buildings performed as investments. Ian Cullen was instrumental in researching this survey and from his experience on the project, he considers that there is no evidence of reluctance to invest in modern buildings if they are, like traditional listed buildings, in a suitable location and attract a good quality of tenant thus showing the possibility of high rental value. As with all listed buildings the listing would only discourage investment if it was so strict that the building could not be easily adapted for use.

Britain has one of the most developed property markets in the world. Australia and America are proportionately less developed in this area given their considerable size. France, Holland and Germany are slightly less advanced in property than Britain but Southern Europe has a long way to go. How are countries with less capital ex-

pected to fund the expensive business of maintaining their important postwar buildings? Will the result be that the architectural heritage of the modern era will not be represented properly in these countries? Drawing from their efforts to preserve the earlier MoMo (Modern Movement) architecture, such countries can be expected to use voluntary help to document buildings as an alternative to preservation. War damage also has to be considered. In Croatia documentation is a priority. Voluntary consulting on various structural and technical issues has been adopted in Estonia where the first version of a national MoMo Register is being collated.

Tourism related revenue might apply to those countries above which are safe to travel in. Revenue generated by tourism and related activities is central to the Chairman of the Arts Council, Peter Palumbo's argument for investing in restoration. He claims that in Britain, 'there is much evidence that expenditure on the arts, pound for pound, generates more Vat and related revenue and increases the return to the Treasury'.

The Millennium Commission is one possible area of funding in Britain. The National Lottery will have a turnover of £2 billion a year, the proceeds of which could provide an endowment fund of approximately £10m annually, the income from which could be used for maintenance and refurbishment or for new buildings. Nick Wates' article in the new magazine, *Perspectives* suggests that one of the initiatives could be 'The restoration and celebration of Britain's main architectural and planning contributions to international culture, such as the Neo-Classical city, the landscape garden, the country house'. From the tone of this we can expect this Commission to become a prime battle ground for the Prince versus the 'architects'.

At the time of going to press, DOCOMOMO and the Twentieth Century Society are campaigning for English Heritage to reconsider their recent decision to remove Erno Goldfinger's Alexander Fleming House from their list of proposals. This is a typical example of the politics of preservation. The building is – unpopular with the public, 'important' in the eyes of architectural historians and the motive for its removal from the proposal list has been put down to politics. English Heritage denies this, claiming that they are delaying a decision until they assess whether the building fulfilled its original brief. It will be interesting to see which side will win this particular argument.

Katherine MacInnes

ABOVE: Stanley Clark Heston and Charles Fish, Prototype McDonalds 1953, Downey, California (listed). Photograph: The Journal of Preservation Technology; BELOW: Erno Goldfinger, Alexander Fleming House 1962-67, London (under consideration by English Heritage). Photograph: English Heritage

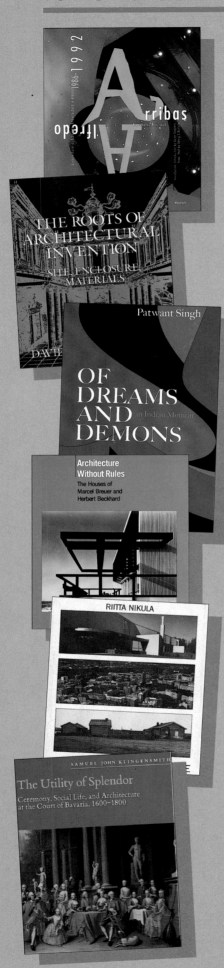

ARRIBAS Arquitectos Asociados by Georg C Bertsch, Wasmuth, 255pp, colour ills, HB DM 168

In his introduction, Oscar Tusquets asks why Barcelona seems to produce a stream of interesting artists. His reasons include the charismatic figure of Gaudi, the city's frontier position and its cosmopolitan character. However he concludes that the root cause is the way in which young designers are trained after graduation. In America, Tusquets argues that the gulf between real building and academic architecture widens. Rather than going back into the theory of design 'young Catalans' seek practical experience and wait for a break. Alfredo Arribas is a perfect example of this system, 'his eruption on to the Spanish architectural scene has been overwhelming: international reaction was instantaneous and enthusiastic'. Alfredo Arribas' interior design shows an interest not only in the aesthetic by the environmental integrity of his careful schemes. He draws from a wide variety of sources: Baroque or minimalist forms, contrast of materials, use or craftsmanship or any other resource that may serve to give shape to the expressive quality of his surprising creations.

THE ROOTS OF ARCHITECTURAL INVENTION Site, Enclosure, Materials by David Leatherbarrow, Cambridge University Press, 235pp, b/w ills, HB £40

This is part of a series of Monographs on Anthropology and Aesthetics of which we have already reviewed *Dance as Text: Ideologies of the Baroque Body* by Mark Franko. Each book analyses historical texts, this one looks at those of L B Alberti, G Semper, A Loos, and Le Corbusier in order to determine their influence on current thinking. Outlining topical thinking in architecture, with reference to rhetoric and the art of memory, *The Roots of Architectural Invention* defines architecture as a form of representation that is caught up in the temporal unfolding of human events. Such profound statements as 'If you take away from a living being action, and still more production, what is left but contemplation?' (Aristotle, *Nicomachean Ethics)* and 'Truth is nothing more than the daughter of time' (Leonardo da Vinci, *Note-*

books) serve to provoke us to draw comparisons between historical roots of architecture and the invention that is manifested today.

OF DREAMS AND DEMONS An Indian Memoir, by Patwant Singh, Gerald Duckworth & Co Ltd, 206pp, HB £16.99

The thrust of this impassioned account by the former editor of India's *Design* magazine is that it provides a crucial, incisive and absorbing analysis of the condition of this provocative country; disentangling and clarifying the web of events that resulted in India becoming 'a cultural amputee severed by all that is best in her'. It unfolds, in autobiographical form, the complex layers that make up the rich cultural mosaic of India. Chronicling her first forty-six years of independence, colonial India – revealed through the eyes of a child equally in awe of the sweet stalls as by the construction work in the imperial city – gives way to the dream of independence, the Nehru era, the turbulence and carnage unleashed during the Gandhi years, and the coming-of-age of the BJP. Concurrently, this vital exposition engages the reader with amusing anecdotes. Fascinating perspectives, *inter alia,* involve architects Philip Johnson, Peter Blake and Basil Spence.

ARCHITECTURE WITHOUT RULES The Houses of Marcel Breuer and Herbert Beckhard by David Masello, WW Norton, 171pp, colour ills, HB £22

The historic collaboration of innovative architects Marcel Breuer and Herbert Beckhard created a radical new type of American housing from the 1950s through the 1970s. Its characteristics, as described and lavishly illustrated here, included more space with less mass; attention to the homeowner's individual needs; avoidance of extraneous decoration; a new balance between the elements of structure, pure form, and function; and intimate relationships between the interior and the exterior natural setting. Breuer, internationally famous for such important public buildings as the Whitney museum of American Art in New York and for such smaller-scale triumphs as the virtually ubiqui-

tous 'Breuer' chair, thrived on experimentation. The younger Beckhard sought Breuer out as mentor and together they designed houses that were asymmetrical, reflecting their conviction that houses should be built for human beings not machines.

ARCHITECTURE AND LAND-SCAPE Buildings of Finland by Riitta Nikula, Otava Publishing Company Ltd, Helsinki, 160pp, b/w ills, PB N/A

Seventy per cent of Finland is forested and unbuilt; some 10 per cent is covered by water. Finnish architecture has been influenced by a wide range of styles. Riitta Nikula suggests that the strength of Finnish Modernism is derived from the fact that the Finns 'never grew up in the midst of varied historical architecture'. Indeed the traditional chapter examined in the first half of the book shows a richness and diversity that belies the contrasting influences that its strategic position on the boarder of East and West afforded it. Their project for the Seville Pavilion in 1992 was a sculptural and ascetic work consisting of a wooden keel, a metal machine and a dramatic interstice and it demonstrates, according to Nikula that 'Finnish architecture truly still is creative by nature'.

THE UTILITY OF SPLENDOUR Ceremony, Social Life and Architecture at the Court of Bavaria, 1600-1800 by Samuel John Klingensmith, University of Chicago Press, 320pp, b/w ills, HB £35.95

The grand palaces and princely villas of the Bavarian Wittelsbach dynasty – Nymphenburg, Schleissheim, the Residenzschloss in Munich, and others – impress modern-day visitors with their complex arrays of great halls and intimate cabinets, their dramatic stair-halls and seemingly endless rows of sumptuously decorated rooms. But these dazzling residences did not exist solely to delight the eye. Klingensmith discusses how, over the years, successive rulers reshaped the internal space of their residences to reflect changes in the elaborate ceremonial that regulated every aspect of daily life at court. The intricacies of Bavarian court practice are investigated and

the author demonstrates that Versailles was only one among several influences on German palace planning.

UNDERSTANDING ARCHITECTURE THROUGH DRAWING by Brian Edwards, E & FN Spon imprint of Chapman and Hall, 185pp, b/w ills, PB £17.95

The introduction to this book claims that the 'act of drawing is an important starting point for the intellectual process that we call 'design'. The two functions of drawing are firstly recording and analysing existing examples and secondly a medium for testing imagined objects. Freehand and technical drawing are two interpretations of the skill which every architect must acquaint themselves with. Between these two opposites there are a range of subtle differences. This book follows subjects from 'Perspective' and 'Line and Shade' to case studies in drawing such as 'Towns, Townscapes and Squares'. Drawing techniques and mental approaches to the problem of translating 3D apply to the technique of drawing and therefore have equal application to computer 'pages' and to those of a sketch pad.

WALTER PICHLER Drawings, Sculpture, Buildings, introduction by Friedrich Achleitner by Princeton Architectural Press, 204pp, colour ills, HB N/A

From his 1965 exhibition with Hans Hollein to his recent exhibitions at the Hirshhorn Museum and the Museum of Modern Art, Austrian artist Walter Pichler has remained a world-wide inspiration to architects as diverse as Morphosis, Arata Isozaki, Coop Himmelblau, Peter Wilson and Neil Denari. Peter Cook writes, 'The power of Pichler's drawings is undeniable [with] their oscillations between tight precision and atmospheric scribbles . . . As with other Austrian art, Pichler's is highly symbolic, ritualistic, even shocking'. Pichler's intensely energetic drawings form the basis of his sculptures and subsequently the architecture built to house them, blurring the distinction between art and architecture. Friedrich Achleitner's introductory essay explores Pichler's work in relation to his home in St Martin.

ROBERT STACY-JUDD Maya Architecture, The Creation of a New Style, by David Gebhard, Capra Press, 166pp, colour ills, PB £24.99

This biography covers Stacy-Judd's English childhood, his first buildings in North Dakota, and his maverick flowering across the cultural and architectural landscape of Southern California. He saw himself as a pioneer architect akin to the earlier settlers of the East and Midwest. However this image was partly justified because he led an expedition into the Yucatan at the time when Lindbergh crossed the Atlantic. Stacy-Judd's buildings created a sensation in the 20s and 30s with their use of pre-Columbian forms and motifs, Mayan and Aztec structures, and brilliant colours – bright greens, raspberry pinks, hot yellows. This investigation into the genuine nature of his claims of having been inspired by a scholarly study of early Indian archaeology, seems to conclude that the Stacy-Judd had a gift for self publicity rather than modesty, which defy cultural stereotype.

FOUNDATIONS OF ARCHITECTURE An annotated Anthology of Beginning Design Projects by Owen Cappleman and Michael Jack Jordan, Van Nostrand Reinhold, New York, 205pp, b/w ills, PB £26

This book begins with some advice from Henry David Thoreau 'If you have built castles in the air, your work need not be lost; that is where they should be. Now put the foundations under them'. An overview and history of beginning design is provided with illustrations of projects from the students of 25 Universities. The second section gives two-page synopses of all of the projects featuring marginal annotations drawn from various sources, including editorial observations and ideas. The next three major sections contain more specific data varying from detailed programme notes and supplementary information about each project to brief biographies of the authors of some of the projects. A summary in Section 2 provides an easy way of locating a project that is of interest. However, the authors suggest that 'the reader could simply read the book from beginning to end'.

OTTO WAGNER Reflections on the Raiment of Modernity edited by Harry Francis Mallgrave, published by the Getty Centre for the History of Art and the Humanities, 422pp, b/w ills, PB £29.95

A traditionalist designer with imperial ambitions or an avant-garde general leading the charge of a modernist assault, a Secessionist architect with a penchant for iconography or a materialist proponent of realist values – Otto Wagner can be portrayed in many ways. This book is focused less on the visually seductive aspects of Wagner's creations than on the social, intellectual and artistic framework within which the architect brought his works to fruition. The result is a broad, but at the same time concentrated, exploration of the parameters of Wagner's tectonic expression – a canvas of a period in which the sensualist aesthetic tendencies of the late nineteenth century merged with the more *sachliche* vision of 20th-century art.

HAFEN HAMBURG Situations and Objects by Hans Meyer-Veden, Ernst & Sohn, 167pp, b/w ills, DM 98

Hamburg and the harbour of Hamburg were in former times designated as the 'Gateway to the world'. In his notes on Hans Meyer-Veden's photographic investigations 'Vanishing Lines and Perspectives of another Harbour-Time', Frank Werner suggests that there are few more fertile hunting grounds for the photographer than the harbour. The impact of Meyer-Veden's photographs lies in his ability to play objects off one another in a faintly surrealist manner. Werner quotes Samuel Johnson who recognised that 'mental agility, wit, lies in the assumed association of ideas, in the discovery of hidden relationships between images that are outwardly far apart'.

The caption to the first image on page 11 of Architecture in Arcadia, AD Vol 63, no 5/6, was incorrect. The above image is of George Oldham. The publishers apologise for this mistake.

ARCHIGRAM

The significance of Archigram's work for the international community of architects has long been recognised. This London based group anticipated the global interrelatedness of culture and technology. Their futuristic ideas are back in the focus of debates about future urban life once again.

Ron Herron, Peter Cook and Dennis Crompton have developed a sophisticated spatial structure arranging Archigram's work into a coherent whole. The exhibition includes more than 200 original drawing, over a dozen models, former concepts which have been partially translated into reality and reconstructions of shows.

The Archigram group was formed by Warren Chalk, Peter Cook, Dennis Crompton, David Greene, Ron Herron and Michael Webb. Their ideas responded to space travel and moon landing, subculture and The Beatles, science fiction and the new technologies of the 60s and 70s. Their historical inspiration came from artist/architects such as Buckminster Fuller, Bruno Taut and Friedrich Kiesler. They created radical alternatives to cities, houses and other architectural arche-types. The pluralism of their architectonic vocabulary is demonstrated through collages of advertising symbols from the world of consumer goods, conglomerates of cities reminiscent of spaceships, or meta-phors drawing on robotics and organistic Cities. Their radical re-definitions of flats as 'capsules' and of cities as 'Walking Cities' or 'Plug-in Cities' (both 1964) produced a formal aesthetic vocabulary that went beyond functionalism. Their ideas influenced contemporary art and subsequent avant-garde architecture in Austria, Japan, Italy and America.

Kunsthalle, Vienna Feb11-May1 ,1994 George Pompidou in Paris, June 22 onwards. A book about Archigram will be published later on this year by Academy Editions.

STUDIO 333 AT GRONINGEN

In the light of the present controversy surrounding the vulnerable position that architects are forced into by the increasing number of competitions, the Europan venture seems to provide an encouragingly positive alternative. Europan is a European federation of national organisations which manage architectural competitions with a view to creating real building projects and helping young architects in Europe to develop and promote their ideas. Unfortunately Britain does not subscribe to Europan, a fact which has become increasingly ironic since the recent 1994 award for the Groningen site was given to the London based, Studio 333.

Studio 333's interpretation of the Europan theme 'at home in the city, urbanising residential neighbourhoods' is manifested through a reassessment of the possibilities of flexible living. The site was treated as a complex of three different elements: Attractors (locations for key public functions); Condensers (social and service amenities) and Mediators (elements of transition and interaction). It seeks to resolve the relationship between natural and urban space once separated in this area by the old city walls and the, now obsolete, industrial urbanism. These elements are implemented under the cultural context of 'circus living' which aims to revitalise this intermediate place.

On a specific level, Studio 333 concentrated on responding to the increasingly ambiguous relationship between work and home. A flexible space called a 'winter garden' is an integral part of every 'condenser' unit or 'domestic factory' and can be extended into, in order to create a space ratio that suits the specific needs of each user. The winter garden can be used as an external space with large windows that open and close. It can be appropriated by associated rooms and functions or it may simply contain an independent function.

PERSPECTIVES

In his speech at the launch of the new magazine *Perspectives*, Prince Charles claimed that he was a 'great believer in artistic freedom' but that since the 'psychologicial impact of the built environment is enormous' there is a need for a magazine which gives the general public 'a voice and a view'. Contrary to expectations, it is the built environment rather than architecture that the first issue seems to focus on – motorways, towns and energy-producing systems.

Although Rowan Moore of *The Telegraph*, considered that this broad overview manifested itself in a confusing lack of direction, to others the direction seems clear – through *Perspectives* Prince Charles aims to 'recreate a spirit of *this* age'. This raises the question of a consensus, which brings us dangerously close to the carbuncle saga begun in '89. Should it be the spirit of modernism or the 'community' spirit, that shapes our built environment – how do we avoid the mediocre conclusion which decisions made according to the common denominater so often reach.

This picture of Prince Charles talking to Sir Norman Foster and Michael Hopkins at the launch party may be interpreted as a reconciliation. But, just as one could assume that Grimshaw's Waterloo Terminal on the front cover of the launch issue might signify an endorsement of modernism, the text compares it firmly to a continuation of Pugin's philosophy and to the craftsmanship of the Gothic builders. So the healthy debate continues, although the Prince was at pains to confirm that he wanted to 'heal divisions not create more'.

Instead of reinforcing long held views, the magazine could adopt an educative role and provide a forum to allow both the public and the architects to have a voice. If *Perspectives* succeeds in this mutually beneficial constructive vein then it will, indeed be the magazine that 'we have all been waiting for'.

A DIFFERENT HOUSE – GERMAN AND AUSTRIAN ARCHITECTURE 1890–1938 IN MORAVIA AND SILESIA

The vitality of the competing debates about art and architecture, form and function and the classical heritage during the late 18th and early 19th century, has ensured the legacy left in this part of central Europe is relevant to us today. Open plan living areas, the use of the dividing wall, the geometric cube – are revealed as contentious, novel and fought over by the competing schools adhered to by many of the pupils of Otto Wagner whose work is included. Through its use of plans, drawings and photographs of interiors and exteriors, and models, the book gives a vital sense of the actual physical reality of these domestic spaces.

Mies van der Rohe is represented by his Villa Tugendhat of 1930 – its open plan living room curtained off by a screen of ebony. All that is missing is colour to pick out the acid green of the cowhide upholstery. Olbrich's Cafe Neidermeyer is there with its lacy metal work, and Adolf Loos' 1917-18 house near Brno. Joseph Hoffman's richly eclectic style is also present, totem pole interior in one building and exterior striping on another.

The curator, Dr Jindřich Vybíral, singles out the work of the underestimated Leopold Bauer (Born in Krnov 1872, died Vienna 1938). His Villa Reissig, Brno 1902 and Villa Kurze, Krnov 1902-3 (left) were billed at the time as some of the first modern houses in Austria. There is a silent though visible influence of the approach to architecture demonstrated in the English house. This show of modernist domestic architecture follows the exhibition of Czech cubism that travelled to Paris last year, revealing more of the fascinating culture of this area of central Europe. (Verina Glaessner). *Exhibition in Prague's St Agnes Convent and in Brno. Mounted by the Czech National Gallery with help from the Goethe Institute and the Austrian Cultural Institute.*

A NEW TATE GALLERY FOR MODERN ART?

Richard Burdett, Director of the Architecture Foundation, chaired the first in a series of Forums to consider contemporary architecture for museums and galleries as a prelude to the Tate's own plans for a Tate Gallery of Modern Art. He opened the discussion with the question of the conflict of interests between architects and artists, suggesting that artists prefer exhibiting in low key conversions such as the Saatchi Gallery on Boundary Road but that architects prefer new spaces like the Hans Hollein Museum in Salzburg, Austria.

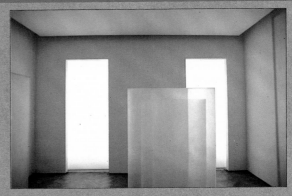

The Stanton Williams presentation emphasised the use of alternate natural and artificial light to pull visitors through the space. They use permeability and transparency to focus views through volumes such as staircases and the play of light on different textures to create the spirit of the space. Lights are often oblique where the glare is bounced off an adjacent surface as in the Gas Works, Birmingham which is one of few galleries with natural side-lighting crucial for illuminating 3D works.

The artist, Ben Hancock questioned the quality of light used in large galleries such as the Sainsbury Wing of the National Gallery by Venturi Scott Brown, which he felt did not show pictures to their best advantage and that stronger natural light should be used. Paul Williams suggested that the conservation rule dictated low light levels but a representaitive from the Tate Gallery argued that we should not have such a passive idea of conservators restrictions and that such problems could be approached laterally by subtracting the amount of time spent in storage.

The images chosen by Evans and Shalev for Tate Gallery West in St Ives focused on a sensitivity to site since the gallery's *raison d'etre* is to show the Tate's St Ives collection where it was created. The specific rather than general spaces are in character with the local architecture and the building's orientation uses the site since the central drum acts as a sea shell to amplify the noise of the sea. The drum also acts as a theatre and allows natural light into each gallery but it reduces the display area of the building to about 35% of the total area. David Shalev maintained that this is why the building is alive and Eldred Evans argued that the small galleries provide a domestic scale for the pictures which were mostly conceived for that context.

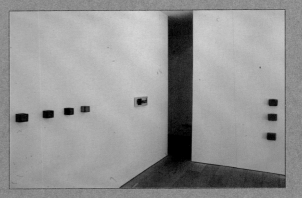

By comparing the exhibition layout of the Tate in the 60s to a contemporary Ben Nicholson show, Julia Peyton-Jones, Director of the Serpentine Gallery, reminded the audience of the changes that have occurred in the last 20 years and the overwhelming need for 'form follows function' and flexibility in any design. She disagreed with Evans's 'domestic context' theory and said that there was no excuse for the overcrowding that this solution caused. She argued that with the development of video images, rotating screens, installations and performance art, galleries were having to approach the question of space in a different way. She reinforced this view by illustrating a recent example where the work of Agnes Martin and Mona Hatoum, both with contrasting light and space requirements, was exhibited consecutively in the same space.

Through visiting a selection of contemporary art galleries and museums internationally, Claudio Silvestrin had reached the conclusion that most of these buildings were a monument to architects rather than to artists. The Parthenon, he argued, was not an architectural masterpiece but a temple masterpiece and, in the same way, galleries should be designed around visual orientation to the art. By using simple forms, clear exhibition rooms, neutral floors and humbling imperfections in details, the architect should be able to defer the structure to the art for which it exists. Alan Stanton argued that pure neutrality was not the ultimate solution in the light of the layered response any building was required to make to its environmental context and to the occupiers.

FROM ABOVE: White Cube Gallery, St James's, London, 1993; Hugh Williams Gallery, Mayfair, London, 1987; Victoria Miro Gallery, Mayfair, London, 1991

ARCHITECTURE OF TRANSPORTATION

INGENHOVEN OVERDIEK PETZINKA, CIRCULAR TERMINAL FOR THE COLOGNE/BONN AIRPORT, GERMANY

Architectural Design

ARCHITECTURE OF TRANSPORTATION

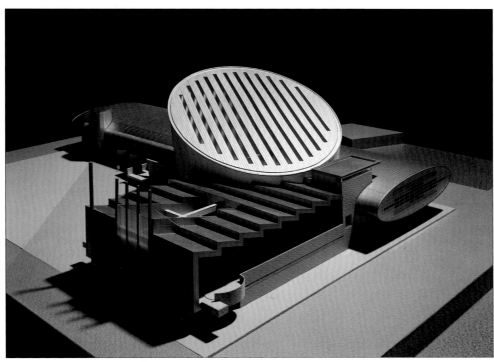

SHIN TAKAMATSU, NAGASAKI FERRY TERMINAL, KYUSHU, JAPAN; *OPPOSITE*: FENTRESS BRADBURN / BHJW,
MAIN PASSENGER TERMINAL, DENVER INTERNATIONAL AIRPORT, COLORADO

ACADEMY EDITIONS • LONDON

Acknowledgements

We would like to thank Cezary Bednarski for his input into this issue; all the architects who contributed to the Travelling Architects: William Alsop, Studio Asymptote, Van Berkel & Bos, Ian Ritchie, Shin Takamatsu, Lebbeus Woods; and a special mention to Martha Rosler who kindly permitted us to use her essay, *In the Place of the Public; Observations of a Traveller* taken from *The Invisible in Architecture*, edited by Ole Bouman and Roemer van Toorn, Academy Editions, February 1994; Erica Sheene for her clarification on Shin Takamatsu.

Front Cover: Odile Decq and Benoit Cornette, Control Tower and Technical Block, Bordeaux Airport; *Inside Covers:* Paul Lukez, Traces of the Artery, Boston

Photographic Credits

All material is courtesy of the architects unless otherwise stated:
Jerry Butts *p2*; Paolo Rosselli *p6*; Cezary Bednarski *pp22-27*; Centre Audio Visuel SNCF *p26 above*; Adrian Velicescu *p38*; Katherine Demetriou: *pp40-41*; Christophe Valtin *pp48-49*; Ron Johnson *p50*; Richard Davies *pp54-57*; Jo Reid & John Peck *pp5, 60, 62, 63 above right and left, 65*; European Passenger Services: Paul K Childs *p64*; Keith Collie and Mick Thomas *p65 below*; Michel Denance *pp74-76, 79 above*; Emanuela Minetti *p77 centre*; Peter Cook *p80*; John Linden *pp82-83*; Eamonn O'Mahony *p84*; Toshiyuki Kobayashi *pp3, 86*; Retoria *pp88, 90-91*

EDITOR: Maggie Toy
EDITORIAL TEAM: Iona Spens, Rachel Bean, Pip Vice, Katherine MacInnes
ART EDITOR: Andrea Bettella CHIEF DESIGNER: Mario Bettella
DESIGN TEAM: Meret Gabra-Liddell, Owen Thomas

CONSULTANTS: Catherine Cooke, Terry Farrell, Kenneth Frampton, Charles Jencks
Heinrich Klotz, Leon Krier, Robert Maxwell, Demetri Porphyrios, Kenneth Powell, Colin Rowe, Derek Walker

First published in Great Britain in 1994 by *Architectural Design* an imprint of
ACADEMY GROUP LTD, 42 LEINSTER GARDENS, LONDON W2 3AN
Member of the VCH Publishing Group
ISBN: 1-85490-240-7 (UK)

Contents

SIR NORMAN FOSTER AND PARTNERS, NEW AIRPORT AT CHEK LAP KOK, HONG KONG

ARCHITECTURAL DESIGN PROFILE No 109

ARCHITECTURE OF TRANSPORTATION

EDITORIAL
MAGGIE TOY

The implications of increased travel across the planet, and beyond, have had an unprecedented impact on the nature of our built environment. The need for increasingly more efficient transport interchanges has created a demand for buildings which not only provide the required ease of movement but also celebrate the sense of arrival and departure. The consequences of this increased mobility have made an impact, not only on the architecture created for the interchange but on the shape of our cities which have had to adapt to the extensive use of the car and to the necessity of becoming a part of the global village. Through transport, our cities have become larger and the Earth has become effectively smaller. The need to be adjacent to efficient forms of transport has influenced urban plans.

Increased travel opportunities and more numerous connections to correspondingly more termini have brought into focus the demand that travel makes on our time. Time spent in travel is the state of being neither here nor there and thus non productive. We demand that every effort be made to minimise this inconvenience and maximise time use. The concept of time-travel becomes particularly poignant when travelling by air; the notion that you can arrive somewhere before you set off is an appealing one for many, but as yet HG Wells and 'Quantum Leap' are one step ahead of our capabilities.

Although we are still unable to travel in time there are many options open to us. Whenever making a journey – whether by foot, car, bus, train, plane or boat – a variety of changeover points is encountered. Each of these has different requirements, responding not only to necessity but also to our expectations. Travel used to be an experience for which one would prepare, an occasion for which one would dress. Many writers and artists have portrayed successfully the emotion evoked when waving-off a boat or boarding a train. Whilst the sensations are no longer the same, travel still needs preparation and interfaces of transportation are no less emotive environments. Architecture responds not only to the era in which it is designed but also to the nature of transport it interchanges.

Martha Rosler examines the notion of air travel and the range of spaces through which one can emerge. Stations and harbours have a history which designers have to accommodate, but airports do not have this 'emotional baggage' and therefore encourage more freedom in design. Nicholas Grimshaw's Waterloo Terminal building relies upon computer systems in its design, yet,

as Kenneth Powell explains, sits well next to the original Victorian building. Santiago Calatrava, restricted by historic typology, has achieved a 'modern classic' with his comparatively small station in Zurich – capturing the sense of performance with the dramatic canopies and engaging subway link. Cezary Bednarski discusses general concepts facing planners of transport systems and the success achieved by architect/planner, turned politician, Jamie Lerner, in Curitiba, when installing the 'Integrated Transportation Network'.

A selection of 'Travelling Architects' reveals their views on the transport interchanges encountered in transit. Ian Ritchie explains the excitement he demands from the building whilst Will Alsop expresses his frustration at being forced to 'waste' time when travelling. Meanwhile, Lebbeus Woods feels in suspension within the boundaries of an airport.

The contemporary 'Urban Gateway' has increased vitality as we move into the new age of the 21st century. The dynamics of this are examined and the pragmatics explored through a selection of exciting and innovative projects. Odile Decq and Benoit Cornette demonstrate, through their control tower for Bordeaux airport, the design freedom associated with air travel. The design for an office slung underneath a highway indicates the possibilities that surround even our most accepted form of transport and a recognition of economic requirements with an exquisite use of limited space. A 'futureport' by Shin Takamatsu facilitates the docking of a variety of transport systems, a necessary provision projecting from present requirements.

A key element in designing for travel is the availability of information that is comprehensible to those unversed in the same language. The availability of information has to be shared in a universal fashion. Foucault posits that information is used to organise and control people. This is borne out in the transport interchange where the more information given – and, perhaps more importantly, received – the greater the efficiency and speed with which the system can work, the happier the travellers and the greater the control being exerted by the 'authorities'.

The ventures into cyberspace – a space that does not actually exist – may pose quite a different problem for architects and travellers of the future. Perhaps this is ultimate control and ultimate freedom in one. Since no travel is required in cyberspace, the body remains stationary leaving the mind to create a new 'space' through which travellers can experience their own space creations and journey without limitation.

Santiago Calatrava, Lyons Airport Railway Station, France

MARTHA ROSLER

IN THE PLACE OF THE PUBLIC
Observations of a Traveller

*You've the effrontery to tell me I must go to
Kansas City to get to New Orleans. You people
are rewriting geography! You're mad with power.
(An irate traveller in Arthur Hailey's novel Airport,
New York, 1968)*

*Capitalism and neo-capitalism have produced an
abstract space that is a reflection of the world of
business on both a national and international
level, as well as the power of money and the
'politique' of the state. This abstract space
depends on vast networks of banks, businesses
and great centres of production. There also is the
spatial intervention of highways, airports and
information networks. In this space, the cradle of
accumulation, the place of richness, the subject
of history, the centre of historical space, in other
words, the city, has exploded.* (Henri Lefebvre)

As a teenager in the 50s I sailed the
Atlantic and Mediterranean a couple of
times. In the 60s and 70s I drove back
and forth across America. Also in the 70s, I
traversed the country in long-distance buses,
experiencing the bald regimentation of passengers that is suggestive of custody for minor
crimes. I photographed these trips in black and
white. By the end of the 70s, with my tickets paid
by various employers and inviters, I had all but
abandoned the buses for aeroplanes. I offer this
history as typical of the possibilities awaiting the
upwardly mobile middle-class city dweller in the
postwar United States.

In the past fifteen years, living an artist's life, I
have found myself flying many times a year. I
found myself in the company of the besuited and
the befurred, of those in trenchcoats carrying
attaché cases and garment bags or those in
leisure-wear toting skis or pedigree dogs. I
discovered that at many small airports the flyers
included the same people who might have been
riding the bus. I changed my black-and-white film
for colour, and my serious 35-millimetre camera
for a less weighty pocket version. I became
interested in the ephemera and experience of this
form of travel, so different in time, space and
(self-) organisation from train and particularly
long-distance bus travel. In a time in which
production in advanced industrial countries is
increasingly characterised by metaphors of
transmission and flow, I am interested in the

movement of bodies through darkened corridors
and across great distances but also in the efface-
ment of the experience of such travel by con-
structs designed to empty the actual experience
of its content and make it the carrier of another
sort of experience entirely. This totalised representation of air travel and its associated spaces
as 'a world apart' is different from that of any other
form of mass transport.

Walter Benjamin, unexpectedly, ends *The Work
of Art in the Age of Mechanical Reproduction* with
a pocket analysis of architecture: 'Architecture
has never been idle. Its history is more ancient
than that of any other art, and its claim to being a
living force has significance in every attempt to
comprehend the relationship of the masses to
art'. 'Architecture', Benjamin continues, 'is
"appropriated" not only through sight but through
touch; it is experienced by the body as presence,
through "distraction", or habitual use, not through
optical contemplation'. He likens the new art of
cinema to architecture, holding out the hope of
the education of the senses and therefore a
means to combat the fascist aestheticisation of
politics through spectacle. Despite the focus of
his essay on the social effects of photography
and film, Benjamin could hardly have anticipated
the invention of virtual reality, a computer simulated 'environment' or 'architecture' that envelops
the spectator in a sensory phantasmagoria
offering apparently spatial, auditory, and tactile
cues – in other words, 'experience'.[1] Virtual
reality, and 'cyberspace', a broader conception
of a computational environment, exists more in
the promise than in the fulfilment; but it is not
news that in the organisation of physical space
and the design of buildings in advanced industrial society there are elements that relinquish
presence or presentness in favour of significa-
tion: the Empire of Signs. Those seeking
cyberspace dream the future by literally moving
space to the plane of the imaginary.

How far can one advance a discussion of air
travel and its associated spaces, structures and
experiences by broaching the subject of virtual
reality? Not far, perhaps. Nevertheless, as the
opening quotation suggests, Henri Lefebvre –
followed by a host of commentators – has shown
how space is produced by the relations of production, mapping political economy onto the
physical world. Cyberspace too, although only a

simulation, is thrown up by the collective imaginary of late capitalism, a translation of Lefebvre's 'abstract space' to an intangible realm. In describing the role of processes of image reproduction in contemporary society, the situationist Guy Debord has pointed out that 'the spectacle', is created by the mode of production and is not a technological accident, not a freely created spectral other world standing against 'the real': 'The spectacle is not a collection of images, but a social relation among people, mediated by images . . . The spectacle cannot be understood as an abuse of the world of vision, as a product of the techniques of mass dissemination of images. It is, rather, a Weltanschauung which has become actual, materially translated. . . The spectacle, grasped in its totality, is both a result and the project of the existing mode of production'.[2] Ultimately Debord and Benjamin are on the opposite sides of the question of technological optimism, but in terms of diagnostics, Debord's proposition that 'this society which eliminated geographical distance reproduces distance internally as spectacular separation' seems equivalent to Benjamin's concept of fascist aestheticisation.

The history of flight is not separate from the history of information management – nor from that of image production and, ultimately, of 'simulation'. An embryonic start toward virtual reality was the flight simulator. As soon as it became practicable, video became part of flight-simulator training, and video and flight simulation have developed in tandem. Air-traffic controllers spend their free time playing video games and are able to handle their jobs only through derealisation: If they thought of the radar blips as *planes* with *people* in them, they say, they would not be able to last a single day. The recasting of movement as information flow is a consequence of excess complexity.

In the brief compass of the present essay, I want to invoke some features of air travel and airports that, among other things, touch on matters of simulation and representation. I frame my discussion not from the point of view of an expert, an outside observer or even a student, but from that of a traveller. That is, a traveller and an artist.

In 1834 the American Transcendentalist poet and philosopher Ralph Waldo Emerson described railroad travel as a salutary drug of sorts, disconnecting the traveller from place and loosening the perception of stability – or the stability of perception: 'One has dim foresight of hitherto uncomputed mechanical advantages who rides on the rail-road and moreover a practical confirmation of the ideal philosophy that Matter is phenomenal whilst men & trees & barns whiz by you as fast as the leaves of a dictionary. As our teakettle hissed along through a field of mayflowers, we could judge the sensations of a swallow who skims by trees & bushes with about the same speed. The very permanence of matter seems compromised & oaks, fields, hills, hitherto esteemed symbols of stability do absolutely dance by you.'[3]

Back home in the States, railroads were soon extended across the 'empty' continent, linking communities and regions together. Emerson wrote, in 1840, six years after his initial euphoria: 'The railroad makes a man a chattel, transports him by the box and the ton, he waits on it. He feels that he pays a high price for his speed in this compromise of all his will. I think the man who walks looks down on us who ride.' Even in his initial account of the train's perceptual effects, Emerson had noted the habituation to this technological marvel that the English – both travellers and roadside observers – had achieved. A century later Charles Lindbergh lamented his own loss of poetic perception resulting from habituation to flight.

All histories of art's responses to technology invoke the early twentieth-century effusions on modernity offered by the Italian Futurists that ended up affirming the technology of death. War – and its pornographic appreciations – helped dampen technological optimism, even among artists, until it was giddily reawakened by the 'global village' of postwar communications technology and, more recently, by cyberspace. These fictive 'spaces' created by instantaneous transmissions are compensatory for the destabilisations and fragmentations – the clichés of urban life – produced by the 'globalisation' of production and of markets. Despite industrial interest in a yet-to-be-realised technology of environmental simulation, at present the play environments of cyberspace are created by and for restive young men who find few places for mastery among actually existing social relations.[4] But even at present the computer and telecommunications networks that join discontinuous actual places into working units create a functional cyberspace, however primitive and lacking in simulation cues. 'The technological universe is impervious to the here and the there. Rather, the natural place for its operations is the entire human environment – a pure topological field, as Cubism, Futurism and Elementarism well understood.'[5] The movements of industry and information that link discrete areas of the world and simultaneously create localised discontinuities in ways of life and daily experience are not most notable for their transitory perceptual effects, and they have their greatest effects on those not aboard the train. The scale of social and psychic fragmentations occasioned by the globalisation of advanced industrial production and distribution is incomparably vaster than those produced by train, plane or space travel; yet these movements of individuals are symptomatic.

After a century of fascination with the ever-increasing speeds of transportation and information, we find speed alone not particularly discomfiting but possibly reassuring. Motion parallax, no longer confusing, is simply another special effect of travel. Unlike one's pet cat, we have learned to cope with rapid passage across the ground and the water, in conveyances powered by complex hidden mechanisms. Jet travel, in contrast, introduces a dislocation or destabilisation so complete that it is as well to suppress the realisation of where one really is in favour of illusion. The development of technological illusionisms has adequately kept pace with the technological development of motion, and it appears that those who have a taste for imagining the future prefer to do so through simulations rather than through anything as normalised and apparently orderly as jet travel.

The possible euphoria of actually flying, of being in flight, is not capitalised on by those whose business it is to keep us from excessive curiosity or from panic while acting as passengers in commercial aircraft. The determinism of speed has no meaning in the sky, and the detachment occasioned by the dream of flying helps organise each person into private space, making us the perfect audience for an in-flight movie, perfect suckers for the unyielding babying inflicted on us by cabin attendants. The illusions that are provided in mid-air replicate the banalities of everyday life, or worse, the experience of institutionalised infancy in an imperfect womb. The dignity of both passenger and attendant is left at the gate.

Look out of the window of the plane during flight. Below is a vague array of generic sights: rivers, mountains, agricultural parcels, towns and cities or cloud cover and horizon. Rising sun, setting sun, a plane or two flying above or below. Except for the occasional wonder of the world, the scene lacks impact, dreamlike but without compelling narrative. You object that a trip across the ocean in a commercial liner is not different, only emptier and longer. But on the ocean one sees the water and the waves, one remembers maps and globes, one recognises one's place in a microcosm with a daily round of events, on a voyage that makes no pretence of instantaneity. Flying says there is no journey, only trajectory. Look at the maps at the back of the airline guide: the arrows dominate the featureless shapes on the map. Less to identify with here than with the image of the globe from outer space.

Denial is a powerful psychological mechanism in air travel as in much of the rest of everyday life. Deny speed and elevation. Deny the thinness of the aeroplane's aluminium skin providing warmth, oxygen, protection. Deny the totality of air crashes, the dangers inherent in ageing air fleets, the possibility of incompetent or inadequate

maintenance. Deny the terror of completely relinquishing control to the hidden men/machines up front. Deny the small chance of hijacking or the larger one of 'pilot error'. Deny the absurdity of the space into which you are shoe-horned. But think about this particular physical space. The bit of social space hurtling through the air that is the aeroplane is regarded by its masters as very expensive real estate, and the smallest margin of comfort above the outrages of cabin class is expensively obtained. (There is a certain historical irony here, since Le Corbusier referred to aeroplanes as little flying houses [!] and attempted to adapt some principles of house design and production from aircraft production.) Even under the best of circumstances, the commercial airliner is much like the least wonderful specimen of long-distance autobus, and certainly is nothing like the ocean liner or even the railroad train, which gather their inhabitants in communal spaces for dining or recreation and do not insist on strapping them to their beds.

One of the great blessings of railroad and then plane travel was the inaccessibility it afforded the traveller: no phones. Now the perpetually plugged-in lower-level executive cannot abandon the telephone, which accompanies him in cars and restaurants and, along with computers and fax machines, into the air. Phones are implanted in seat backs on some aircraft. Fax modems will soon be able to link computers, phones and land terminals with their flying users; the functions, moreover, will likely be combined into a single pocket-size instrument. This telephone slavery completes the circuit of physical passage from point A to point B. As the plugged-in body moves through real space, the plugged-in mind, in the loop of information in transmission, has no respite. How different is this condition from that of the social offender who under house arrest must wear an electronic bracelet? Alternatively, a passenger dons the earphones provided by the cabin attendants or those of a personal Walkman. The interval that might be used for private purposes or socialising, for anything at all, is recast as a duality: produce or consume, work or be distracted. This never-terminated hook-up – an ad hoc version of cyberspace, after all – reflects the auditory horror vacui of all formerly silent public spaces, such as elevators, restaurants and dentists' offices, not to mention nature shows on television, venues that used to be without piped-in sound, a condition of auditory freedom now apparently forbidden – except in terminals, which unlike the aeroplane and the telephone 'hold' mechanism, is not yet deemed conveniently colonisable by 'easy listening'.

Eventually, the plane lands, the traveller arrives. As an invitation to theorising, the airport

ABOVE: Martha Rosler, Untitled, (United, O'Hare), 1990; BELOW: Martha Rosler, Untitled, Philadelphia, 1992

suggests the meeting point of theories of time and of space, of schedules and of layouts. The airport is a multi-dimensional, multi-function system whose overriding concerns are operational. To state the obvious, airport design requires a consideration of a set of flow trajectories in vertical space, a dimension normally regarded as more or less stable. The most intensive period of airport construction coincided with stripped-down functionalist Modernism. It would be interesting to compare airports built in the early postwar period and more recently, when the dominant metaphors of flow dynamics shifted from water to information. Airports, unlike railroad terminals, are not in the heart of an urban milieu but situated out of town and so not subject to the same kinds of siting and façade considerations as other major structures. Furthermore, they are often under the control of different agencies from those responsible for town or city planning. Falling under the reign of the technocrat, they do not encode capital the way large urban structures do. Since the airport is conceived of as a web of functionalities, the idea of an architecturally imposing gateway structure, while certainly present, is secondary. The conception of the façade is also altered by the fact that in the best circumstances airports are approached by ground travellers not from roads but from trains – preferably underground, though this is rarely so in the United States. Increasingly, they are app-roached by people getting off one plane only to get on another. That technical efficiency, not the state of the public, is venerated by the airport and has resulted in structures whose experiencing subjects are atomised. Inside the terminal build-ings, each atomised subject is the same con-sumer created by other commercial transactions: an irrationalist, operating in the realm of desire.

Except for a few high-profile terminals, the airport may not be usefully described in terms of 'architecture'. Airports reflect the thinking of engineers, underlining the historic split that turned architects into a profession of more or less willing mandarins. While the airport does not escape its conception as a system composed of a linked series of operational 'modules' – a term interestingly incorporated not only into the lexicon of space travel but also of the 'architecture' of the computer 'environment' – it is useful to elide the distinction between space that is architected and space that is engineered.

Architecturally, the terminal is conceived as a hangar or shed. Many terminals celebrate the functionality of glass and steel, elements not only held to be essential to the construction of the terminal structure but signalling the fabric of the plane and the act of navigation. Façade elements are de-emphasised in favour of an interior often defined by glass but generally lacking Crystal Palace triumphalism. Central areas or concourses

range from the humdrum to the grandiose, with little in-between. Huge aimless spaces are marked off by rope-and-stanchion arrays to keep order among those lined up at ticket counters. Away from the central hall, acoustic tile in grim tracks, self-effaced flooring, fluorescent-lit low-ceilinged corridors, reductive directional signs no more inflected than road signs – although the latter are meant to be grasped at a high rate of speed – are ubiquitous. The accountant and the crowd-control manager are the gods supplicated within.

At Kennedy Airport, Eero Saarinen's biomorphic 1962 TWA terminal, while attempt-ing an inspiring interior, is probably more comprehensible from the air than from below. Helmut Jahn's celebrated late-eighties United Airlines terminal at Chicago O'Hare Airport, America's busiest, organises our perceptions in a straight ahead interior runway with a big sky. If the great railway terminals created a pseudo-sacral public space with soaringly meaningful overheads, the Jahn terminal is mausoleum-like, a reminder of individual insignificance. And that authoritarian black-and-white chequerboard floor! But Jahn, although predictably megalomaniacal, can be held accountable only for his design, not for its emptiness, which surely is a cultural product rather than simply a personal shortcom-ing. Underground at O'Hare are very dim tunnels linking the terminals, tunnels through which homeless people guide their shopping carts.

The airport is not organised as a signifying space that creates a public any more than the aeroplane itself is – unless we accept the mes-sage of the plane and the terminal equally to be human docility, homogeneity, replaceability, transitoriness. If money and crowd control are the prime movers, surveillance is the constant practice. Surveillance may or may not be accomplished with the aid of hidden cameras. There is always in place some dangerous and invasive Other to be invoked, and every airport now appears organised around the spectre of the international terrorist, a sufficient excuse for the remilitarisation of flight.[6] Especially in certain European capitals, terrorist explosives must be guarded against. Yet ordinary armoured-car robbers of airport payrolls and payments, not to mention baggage thieves and pickpockets, are more likely to be the interlopers at American airports – thieves and those with no homes.[7] One effort of policing terminals is to prevent homeless people from seeking shelter at the airport. In this task the airport managers are fortunate, because airports, unlike ground-transportation terminals, are located well away from urban centres. O'Hare is one of the few US airports that can be easily reached by rail from the city. The airport, like the

ABOVE: Martha Rosler, Untitled, (LAX), 1990; BELOW: Martha Rosler, Untitled, Schiphol, 1992

modern corporate space, cleanly embodies Foucault's observations on the ways that information is used to organise and control people.

Information, a necessity for every traveller, is not easily obtained. With any change in schedule or plans, whether caused by accident, mechanical failure, bomb threat or weather, the system breaks down, and the flow of passengers stops. The oldest model of bureaucracy – information constriction, information sadism – takes over. People stand in long lines or in clumps trying to find out what is occurring, with almost no effort at co-operation from the airline employees, who stand behind counters, manipulating computer terminals, and decline to make eye contact. Hours pass. Food and drink are rarely offered. Sometimes hotel accommodation is offered, but regardless of the nature of the emergency, information is as far as possible withheld.

On the other hand, the search for impersonal information on the part of the authorities extends to a microscopic level. High-technology bomb detectors, 'thermal neutron analysers', have been announced as being readied to search luggage at international gateways in the hunt for plastic explosives. More routinely, all hand luggage (and much checked baggage) is scrutinised by means of x-ray machines and hand searches, and people must pass through magnetic metal detectors or are physically searched. More personally, customs and immigration officers, inspecting people and documents, apprehend illegal entrants and turn them back.

As a teenager I would drive out with friends to Kennedy Airport (then Idlewild) to watch the planes take off and land, but now people who watch planes prefer to do so casually, in the airport bar. Even so the bar is more likely to have no windows facing out. In the airport terminal, pseudo-sidewalk cafes and theme restaurants are common. In the United States, the airport is so far removed from the model of the public plaza or terminal that the fundamental right to solicit money or to hand out political and religious leaflets was uniformly denied until reinstated by the Supreme Court. In this effort at a tidy order free of political or religious displays, airport authorities revealed their conception of the facility as a private space much like a store or a home. 'Public spaces' are rethought as 'non-private' spaces, spaces of consumption and control or spaces of disorder, characterised by homeless people, by crime, vehicular traffic.

In countries less dominated by the reign of commodities, in the peripheral reaches of the Empire of Signs, the totalisation of the airport as singular unified space is less advanced. In Johannesburg, commercial signage is minimal, the modest bit of art is commemorative bronze statuary, and passengers ascend and descend the planes via staircases moved onto the runway.

This is a society in which consumers know themselves, and the State has other preoccupations than facilitating consumption. In the United States, the air-travel market was given free reign by the deregulation process begun in the late 70s. The onset of Reaganism forestalled the minimal protections proposed for small airlines and unprofitable routes. Competitive practices were touted as allowing customers to achieve lower fares on small airlines; instead, increasingly monopolistic control over pricing, scheduling and routing led to higher fares, far fewer airlines and a reduced schedule. The US market, dominated by a few carriers, is an unstable oligopoly.

At US Air's hub in Pittsburgh, a new terminal includes a shopping mall (with regular mall prices, not the usual extortionate air-terminal prices), apparently still the only model to which an air terminal can aspire. The huge terminal also contains a 'meditation room' designed by a New York artist, and works by other internationally known artists, among them Robert Morris. Many US airports incorporate art, much of it mandated under municipal 'percent for art' programmes. A *New York Times* article called attention to the differential between the potential audiences at airports and at museums.[8] Unconcerned with the private property argument about airports, the *Times* treats these works as examples of public art. The article compares Chicago O'Hare airport's sixty million passengers and uncounted other visitors in 1990 to the four and a half million who visited New York's Metropolitan Museum of Art. The elision of the difference between travellers passing art works and paid visitors to a traditional museum tells. What also tells is the article's description of a planned Baudrillardian simulation in the Denver hub in the Rockies: 'the facility will use its multi-million-dollar art budget to bring the essence of Colorado to the many transfer passengers who never venture outside the airport. Among innovations planned are a light sculpture that will cast changing Colorado cloud formations onto an atrium roof, and a 60-foot-long water sculpture reproducing nearby mountain landscapes.

The terminal earnestly approaches the status of the enormous room, the prison-house of culture, described by people as disparate as the poet Cummings and the philosopher Adorno.

This conception of the airport as museum is municipally imposed and does not follow the logic of the resident airlines, which naturally want to colonise your mind with notions of big and little trips. The works of art – often screwed to the wall like fire hoses in thick Plexiglas cases – generally seem negligible, out of place, absorbed into the 'architecture' like inexplicable 'beauty marks' or eruptions on its office-interior skin. Airlines, as I

ABOVE: Martha Rosler, Untitled (TWA,JFK), 1992; BELOW: Martha Rosler, Untitled (London), 1984

have suggested, want terminals to be more like virtual than actual spaces. Airport corridors are generally no better lit than the average department store, with similar intentions – to cast you inward to the psychological space of desire. In the airport, desire is always infinitely deferred, and meaning is elsewhere and otherwise. Back-lit photos lure us to Tahiti or Cincinnati (unless we are in Tahiti or Cincinnati), to Disneyland or the Eiffel Tower, to Marlboro Country or to the land of financial accumulation, telephones and computers or of remote outmoded forms of transportation, such as a canoe trip in rural Africa – sometimes both simultaneously.

'The economic organisation of visits to different places is already in itself the guarantee of their equivalence. The same modernisation that removed time from the voyage also removed from it the reality of space.'[9] Photography and the creation of (commodified) space, which share a common origin, continue to develop together; preservation efforts, always a project of elites, are being carried forward via electronic digitisation of images, the latest linkage of photography and computerisation. *Projet Patrimoine 2001* will photograph 200 'cultural and natural wonders' and make the images 'instantly available worldwide through digital transmission'. What makes this preservation through image appropriation notable is that it is a project of UNESCO, the United Nations Educational, Scientific and Cultural Organisation, under the impetus of its new Spanish director, Federico Mayor. The project will be substantially underwritten by grants from the immensely rich La Caixa Foundation, based in Barcelona and supported by its municipal pension funds. Technical services will be donated by Kodak, France Telecom and the Gamma photo agency. The idea is to make images of endangered treasures before, according to the *New York Times*, 'they are further damaged by war or the environment'. It is important that it is UNESCO initiating this project, which can be of interest only to the advanced industrial countries, because under its previous African director UNESCO was boycotted by them because of its challenge to their control of information. (The US withdrew from UNESCO in 1984.) Under Mayor, UNESCO claims to have turned toward 'universality'. Experience tells us that claims for universality translate into alibis for domination.

Allowed past security checks, ticket holders hurry to the gates. Aeroplanes do not rest like ocean liners in a great public arena, and airport bays and piers do not replicate the docks of ships. Instead, they run up and down terminal buildings placed alongside the runways rather than along the 'natural' juncture of ocean and land. Thus for passengers there is no immediately intuitive logic to the terminal layout, which is often

described in terms of 'fingers'. Such biomorphic analogies notwithstanding, the fingers may be on far too many 'hands' to make obvious sense. Mystification of place and space appears to conflict with the operational aim of routing people efficiently. The passenger must be directed by signage as well as by moving walkways, passageways, and tunnels designated more like the rows in parking garages than like public streets. In the airport, as in the giant shopping mall or immense natural history museum, an aerial schematic map tells you 'You are here'.

As the space of the terminal does not explain itself, so the plane does not beckon. The aeroplane does not match the majestic image of either the big ship or the long-distance train. It is just another information/ transportation module. At best, to stick with metaphor, the plane is likely to call to mind a tiny vessel lost in vastness, a storm tossed boat rather than the iceberg monolith of a big ship with its deep airhorns, rather than the long stretch of a passing train Doppler shifting through space and time. Inside the craft the meanness of space allotted each person, the relentless miniaturisation with no opening into a larger space helps create this image of puniness and fragility. But the interior and the exterior of the plane itself do not coincide. Rather than participating in a grand display of arrivals and departures, air passengers are politely hustled onto and off the planes preferably through 'jetways' channelling them from terminal to plane and vice versa. These elevated walkways share something with the elevated shopping arcades, or skywalks, in malled-in America, although they are narrower – featureless passages perhaps more reminiscent of a birth canal leading from the plane's shrouded entrance. Indeed, the airport itself can be seen as the subterranean erupted upward, a series of blind passages and darkened tubules with walkways moving passengers in an approximation of peristalsis. Out on the field, the aeroplane, with its female name, lies quiescent, serviced by shuttling fuel tankers and 'honey wagons', food trucks and cargo carriers. These evocations of the body are the closest approach to the possibly female in the phallocratic regime of flight.[10] That it calls to mind structures of domination replicates the relationship of air travel to the land, to the sky and to the earth itself.

What of the airport as a gross physical, a geographic, entity? Airports are tremendous colonisers, rendering the land they occupy and the surrounding areas into wasteland. Like the ground under a city, the airport bulldozes and flattens out the spaces of nature. It brings the land as close as possible to the condition of perfection, in which geometry has conquered diversity or incident. Air travel wrecks more than

Jan Benthem, Mels Crouwel and Khio Liang le Associates, extension to Amsterdam Airport (Schiphol), 1993

the land on which the airport sits; aside from the chemical pollutants inevitably introduced into the surrounding landscape, human and animal life in a wide area around the airport is disturbed by airport noise. But money talks, and pilots are often required to loop about in the air, giving up a direct route in or out of the airport in order to preserve the quiet of wealthy homeowners below. Land values around airports and in the flight path are depressed, and working-class dwellers are annoyed and sometimes killed by overflights.

When catastrophe befalls a plane carrying a large number of Americans, when such a plane crashes or blows up, routine is left behind. Along with emergency services, news and information are marshalled for various purposes. 'The machinery of containment is deployed by the airline and the State, human interest stories are written and grief is exploited by news agencies, blame is sought as a cathartic act. With crashes of international flights, the rationalist efforts of state agencies are offset by sudden suspicions of conspiracy and secret terror. Pilot error, the preferred explanation, is not particularly reassuring to travellers, traffic-controller mistakes or mechanical failure even less so. Foreign acts of aggression may suit State purposes. Worst are the suspicions or confirmation of sabotage. Sabotage, formerly perpetrated by persons seeking life-insurance gains, is now inescapably the purview of international terrorists, almost all Islamic. Mass paranoia, generally repressed, surges around such incidents, fuelled by the families of victims, who brush aside explanations offered by the State. As time passes, the families' dragnet is cast wider and wider, invoking secret plots and counterplots by intelligence and other, unnamed clandestine forces, involving explosives and drug smuggling, agents and double agents. This was as true of the Soviet downing of KAL flight 007 over Sakhalin in 1983 as of the still-unresolved bombing of Pan Am Flight 103 over Lockerbie in 1988 and the crash of the military charter flight over Gander in 1985.

Airports, like all modernising modalities, serve the needs of capital above all and leach away resources from those who are not integrated at a sufficiently high level into the political economy. Just as in suburbia or in inner cities, and on the streets below the skywalks and the outer perimeters of the indoor malls, service workers can be seen waiting for hours at bus stops or riding for hours to and from work, because car ownership is presumed to be 'universal', the ubiquity of air travel underdevelops more modest forms of transportation, such as the railroad and the long-distance bus. Some cities, like St Louis, sink millions into light-rail lines to the airport while neglecting internal transport in the highly segregated city. Lefebvre again: 'Abstract space reveals its oppressive and repressive capacities

in relation to time. It rejects time as an abstraction – except when it concerns work, the producer of things and of surplus value. Time is reduced to constraints of space: schedules, runs, crossings, loads. Time has disappeared in the social space of modernity . . . Economic space subordinates time, whereas political space eradicates it because it is threatening to existing power relations. The primacy of the economic, and still more, of the political, leads to the supremacy of space over time'.[11] The reigning paradigm always casts its meanings back through time; wherever possible those meanings are newly embodied in social practices, in landscape, in the built environment. On the way to the commuter railroad that takes me to work from the 'new' Pennsylvania Station in New York City, an enormous, hideous pit with low ceilinged, dreary areas, uncomfortable in every detail, I pass a series of photographs of the old Beaux Arts-neoclassical Pennsylvania Station (McKim, Mead & White, 1906-10) rased by the Pennsylvania Railroad in 1963. The face presented to the street – the architect's face – of this terminal, meant to replicate the Roman Baths of Caracalla, was that of monumental Classicism and stability. Inside, the 'face' the traveller saw was a soaring hymn to engineering. Without romanticising the 'lost' edifice, one may still invoke this grand advertisement for capital as the epitome of the public space, the physically embodied metaphor of an imperial people – as is the still-standing Grand Central Terminal on the other side of town. In these terminals one realises oneself, for good or ill, as part of a totality. In contrast, in the airport, the space on which the new Penn Station clearly is modelled, everything and everyone is weightless, anomic, and the appeal is to consumerism, not to sociality. There is no middle ground between imperial citizenship and the vacuum. Both terminals, the carceral and the grand, house populations of people who would otherwise have to sleep in the street. Their passage across the landscape is in inverse proportion to the speed of those above them. The space created by capital perpetually re-creates its own underworld, its own space of 'underdevelopment' and immobility, its own wasteland.

. . .*The twentieth century is a century which sees the earth as no one has ever seen it, the earth has a splendour that it never has had, and as everything destroys itself in the twentieth century and nothing continues, so then the twentieth century has a splendour which is its own and Picasso is of this century, he has that strange quality of an earth that one has never seen and of things destroyed as they have never been destroyed.* (Gertrude Stein)

How is it that we are confronted with a choice between the intrusive reminders of capital's aspirations toward domination and the blank-eyed emptiness of nowhere and no-body?

14

Notes

1 The term 'virtual reality' was coined by one of its inventors and promoters, Jaron Lanier. The creation of this simulated body of experiences, which is being developed in conjunction with the military-industrial complex, generally involves the donning of goggles or a helmet with tiny video monitors and a glove containing elements that allow the wearer to see and apparently to touch and manipulate objects not present in the same space or not existing in the real world. (Various developers are hoping to get rid of the wires.) The synchronicity and multiplicity of these cues serves to 'inform' the experiencing subject that s/he is 'in'; the other space. The term 'cyberspace' was coined by the science-fiction writer William Gibson in the mid-1980s in his Neuromancer future-dystopia novels and refers to a vision of an entire world based on computer simulations. There is a certain irony to the fact that these nightmarish and paranoic visions of a future far more bleak and disorienting than Orwell's *1984* are likely to be realised through the intervention of the military. See, among other sources, Michael Benedikt, ed, *Cyberspace: First Steps*, Cambridge 1991.

2 Guy Debord, *The Society of the Spectacle*, Detroit 1970.

3 Emerson's journal entries are cited and discussed in John Kasson, *Civilizing the Machine: Technology and Republican Values in America, 1776-1900*, New York, 1976, pp114-16.

4 One wonders what the implications are of the fact that when the industry in question is information transmission, technological development may arise from an initial beginning in fantasy projection, in the space of desire, rather than in 'reality'-oriented problem solving. Magic versus science, the predict-able antipodean choices. For a consideration of the encoding of computational space as private (real) property, see the discussion of 'hacking' as trespass-ing versus the computer invader as 'a polite country rambler' traversing 'picturesque fields', Andrew Ross, *Strange Weather Culture, Science and Technology in the Age of Limits*, London 1991, p82.

5 Manfredo Tafuri, 'The Crisis of Utopia: Le Corbusier at Algiers', in *Architecture and Utopia: Design and Capitalist Development*, Cambridge Mass, 1976, p129.

6 Realism breaks through the implacable denial of the fragilities of flight when the anti-terrorism 'expert', paid to create a *frisson* in his employers and other listeners, refers to a 747 as 'a tin can full of several hundred hostages at forty thousand feet'.

7 Surveillance, of course, misses the big crimes that are the ordinary accompaniments of big business, ranging from extortion of protection money from freight carriers to the far more significant and successful profiteering at public expense occasioned by the constant building and rebuilding at airports.

8 Suzanne Carmichael, *Stuck at the Airport? Then Look at the Art*, in New York Times, 15 December 1991.

9 Guy Debord, *The Society of the Spectacle*, Detroit 1970, prop 168, np. The frustrating sameness of tourist destinations has been described by Jean Baudrillard and such other commentators as Donald Horne. All these accounts, overstated as they surely are for theoretical effect, point out the homogenisation of culture: the beaten path beats down that which it managed to reach with such difficulty. Erasure of difference always leads to efforts by the coloniser to 'preserve' it, but as a depoliticised, aestheticised set of cultural practices – as a 'destination'.

10 The interior of the plane, however, does little to evoke the female, drawing upon the masculinist realms of the factory and the office.

11 Henri Lefebvre, 'Space: Social Product and Use Value', in JW Freiberg (ed), *Critical Sociology*, New York 1979, p287.

Excerpt from The Invisible in Architecture, *edited by Ole Bouman and Roemer van Toorn, Academy Editions, February 1994.*

Martha Rosler, Untitled (Minneapolis), 1992

KENNETH POWELL
NEW DIRECTIONS IN RAILWAY ARCHITECTURE

The *Building News* declared in 1875 that railway termini and hotels are to the 19th century what monasteries and cathedrals were to the 13th century. With the great new London stations of the period, including St Pancras, Paddington and Liverpool Street in mind, the writer added that 'our metropolitan termini have been leaders of the art spirit of our time'. The railway was the single greatest and most far-reaching innovation of the 19th century, reshaping both town and country and transforming society. It quickly became the prime means of transportation for all classes, a cultural and social as much as an economic force. The railway quickly ceased to be a novelty and became a fact of life. Early stations had an ad hoc look – the passenger terminal at Manchester's Liverpool Road looked like (and was) an adjunct to the commercially more important freight terminal – equipped with the most up-to-date warehouses in 1830s Europe.

Our perception of 19th-century railway architecture tends to be overshadowed by the grandiloquence of the great passenger stations – London's St Pancras, Bombay's Victoria Terminal, the Gare de l'Est, for example. The principal task of the railway was, however, moving raw materials and manufactured goods – this is where railway companies, by and large, piled up profits. The scale of the freight business found expression in sheds and warehouses which were often classic examples of the honest 'functional tradition' of 19th-century design, largely ignored by historians and critics and, in many cases, thoughtlessly destroyed in the face of changing approaches to freight handling. Passenger stations have, inevitably, provided the principal expression of railway architecture.

Railways recast every city they touched. The early stations illustrated in Carroll Meek's classic study of *The Rail Road Station* (1956) are city-edge buildings, like the first London Euston, the Boston & Lowell Railroad's 'Car House' of 1835 or the first terminus at Kassel, Germany. The cities expanded to meet the railway. Later in the century railways became part of an increasingly complex, interwoven pattern of services underpinning the industrial city. New York's Grand Central Terminal (built in 1903-13) is a multi-level complex of remarkable grandeur, yet the tracks are buried far below the vast concourse in a gloomy and some-what oppressive world of their own, as remote from the hub of the station as the aircraft stands at a late 20th-century international airport. The trains, it appears, were tidied away – as if (rather absurdly) only partly relevant to the business of travel, though the construction of Grand Central was one of the engineering miracles of the age.

Despite a remarkable flowering of railway architecture between the wars – Michelucci's Florence Santa Maria Novella, the bombastic Milan Centrale and Cincinnati Union Station (by Fellheimer & Wagner) are amongst the most striking products of that age, alongside the work of Holder and Pick on the London Underground – the 1940s and 50s saw the decline of rail travel, first in the USA then in Europe. Architects and critics were mesmerised by the glamour of air travel and the motor car. When Reyner Banham first went to Los Angeles, he had to learn to drive to have any hope of seeing the city of the future (as it was then perceived). In the USA disuse and demolition overtook many fine passenger stations, most notoriously Penn Central in New York, replaced, despite a vociferous campaign of objections, by a dismal commercial development where the railway's presence seemed almost accidental. The 1960s rebuild of London Euston looked like a second-rate air terminal – the distinctive architectural language which railways had generated seemed to have been lost completely. Even rail systems which were indispensable, like the London Underground and New York Subway, were allowed to atrophy. Design quality evaporated, along with pride in the look of things.

The current resurgence of railways worldwide is partly a response to ecological concerns about the impact of roads and cars, especially in cities, while the advance of new rail technology has made trains competitive with aircraft on medium-haul journeys (for example, Washington-New York, Madrid-Seville, London-Paris, Tokyo-Osaka). The French TGV programme points the way to an integrated high speed rail network in Europe, linked to major intercontinental air gateways. (By 2000, the EC, Switzerland and Austria are likely to have 14,000 kilometres of entirely new or upgraded high-speed lines suitable for the TGV.) Japan is a good example of a relatively small, highly advanced, hugely congested country where rail travel is central to internal communications and railway stations are

OPPOSITE: Liverpool Street Station, combining the old and the new, Architecture & Design Group

17

exploding centres of social and commercial life as well as places to board trains.

Throughout the developed world, new rail systems are being used as the adjuncts of major redevelopment and urban design projects. This phenomenon indicates a movement towards greener, more humanly responsive cities where easy movement is a priority. At the end of the 20th century, the railway is again set to become a revolutionary force. Nineteenth-century railways were driven ruthlessly through cities and communities, and their 20th-century counterparts can be controversial – witness the furore over the TGV line through Provence or the Channel Tunnel link from London to England's South Coast. But the potential of the railway today is to strengthen communities and to reassert threatened social values.

Britain was the first railway nation, with 10,000 miles of track built in the first decade of railway development. Yet British governments in the 20th century have undermined the rail system, while pushing through an extravagant and environmentally damaging road building programme. This makes the renaissance of railway architecture in Britain in the last few years little short of miraculous. Nicholas Grimshaw's Waterloo International Terminus is the flagship of the British railway revival. In the face of public spending cuts and the threat of piecemeal privatisation of the system, British Rail somehow managed to commission and build one of the most impressive stations of the century. Grimshaw's Waterloo has obvious precedents in the great Victorian train sheds. But where the 19th-century builder worked on cleared sites, Grimshaw's site was a long, narrow strip of land alongside the existing, early 20th-century station. Since the British authorities are determined to maintain traditional customs barriers – the Channel is seen as an unchanging barrier against foreigners – Waterloo International has to be a secure, self-contained structure, like an airport. Grimshaw makes good use of the site to slot customs facilities, baggage halls and waiting rooms below platform level – passengers emerge on to the platforms only when the trains are ready for boarding. The lower levels of the building (90 per cent of its total area) are not, however, oppressive or gloomy but lofty and daylit, accessed by a road at the foot of the Embankment on which the station stands. The train shed roof is, of course, the feature which attracts attention and it is a beautiful, elegant performance. Grimshaw has, in effect, imposed the image of a Victorian railway terminus on a building with a very different function. Airport style 'passenger handling' facilities aside, the new Waterloo, in common with new airports, has to provide space for a large area of retailing. Transport is no longer seen in Britain as a public service, but a commodity to be marketed . . . Yet

the station is a significant public building and a statement for cohesive urban design in a part of London which is characterised by urban fragmentation and decay. The hyperbole of its architectural form is excusable.

Grimshaw's Waterloo represents an act of atonement for the 1960s Euston, a building where the image of railway architecture was effectively discarded. Euston was criticised for looking like an airport. Waterloo International is very much like an airport but doesn't look like one. Indeed, its architecture has a romantic elegance which only highlights the plodding solidity of the early 20th-century terminus to which it is attached. The notorious indecision in Britain over the express link to the Channel Tunnel looks all the more incongruous in the context of Grimshaw's Waterloo. The final London terminus for trains from the tunnel will not now be a new station at King's Cross, designed by Norman Foster, but an extended St Pancras. Extending the Victorian engineer WH Barlow's shed will be a major exercise in reconciling conservation and new design – a draft scheme has been produced by Architecture & Design Group. The latter practice is responsible for the major rebuilding of London's Liverpool Street terminus, where the improvement of passenger facilities had to be balanced against the requirement for major commercial development. The eastern half of the Victorian station was completely demolished: new platforms sit under the Skidmore Owings & Merrill-designed office blocks of Broadgate. The western shed was carefully restored and extended, in an unashamedly Victorian manner, though using the most up-to-date glazing technology. The architects succeeded in linking a new internal circulation system to the provision of much increased shopping. The net result is a very considerable gain for the traveller in terms of convenience and comfort. (Liverpool Street is the departure point for trains serving Foster's Stansted.)

The operational parts of Foster's King's Cross would have been entirely subterranean, but the building announced itself on the street by means of a glazed concourse of (even by Foster standards) consummate elegance. With Grade I listed Victorian termini hemming it in on either side, the new structure was designed not to compete with their solid grandeur, nor to express a traditional railway aesthetic, but to embrace instead a dynamic image of travel akin to that of Foster's renowned airport at London's Stansted and forthcoming new airport in Hong Kong. Hong Kong's new Central Station, designed by Arup Associates (with Rocco Design Partners) includes a very large glazed multi-level concourse, a striking 'gateway' and an appropriate end of the line for passengers travelling by the new transit

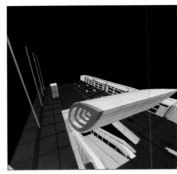

ABOVE: Ellerbe Becket, Vermont Santa Monica Metro, Red Line Station; BELOW: Nicholas Grimshaw & Partners, Waterloo International Terminal

link from the Foster airport. Up to four million square feet of commercial development is, however, planned for the site above the subterranean platforms.

The new airport at Seville by Rafael Moneo – built for the 1992 Expo – demonstrates that Stansted is not the only model for a late 20th-century airport. The interior of Moneo's terminal building has a solid monumentality that takes its cue from the architecture of the basilica and, indeed, the traditional railway terminus. Cruz and Oritz's new Santa Justa Station in Seville, the terminus of the high-speed AVE line from Madrid, equally eschews high-tech show in favour of sleek solidity – this is one of the best new stations since Michelucci's Florence. The success of Sant' Justa owes a good deal to sound planning – the progression into and out of the station, via the arrival area, booking hall and concourse to the platforms is very well handled. The building represents a masterly handling of space. Good planning is also a feature of the transport building designed by Santiago Calatrava. The Stadelhofen railway station in Zurich, completed in 1990, has already acquired classic status. Relatively modest in scale, compared with Waterloo or Seville the station occupies a key site in the city, close to the Opera House square. It was built on an existing track, at ground level, so that the architect's task was to provide comfortable spaces for passengers and an efficient system of circulation to and from the platforms. Calatrava gives the platform canopies a sense of drama and movement. The subway linking the platforms is made into a striking and intense interior, rather than just a way through, encouraging travellers to linger and use the shops and restaurants there. Calatrava's airport station at Lyons-Satolas, now nearing completion, is altogether grander and more ambitious, a key part of the French strategy to link international air travel with the French-inspired TGV system. (Paul Andreu's station at Paris-Charles de Gaulle is part of the same strategy.) There are six platforms enclosed by a 500-metre-long lattice vault. In the centre rises the concourse, a highly expressive, almost exaggeratedly dramatic structure – compared, not without reason, with Saarinen's TWA terminal in New York. Vast, light-filled, Gothic in its splendour, the building will form an unforgettable gateway to France for international travellers, who arrive in the station from the airport via a strongly modelled elevated corridor, a jet age equivalent of the medieval cloister. Calatrava is not especially concerned with the historic typology of railway buildings. The great concourse at Lyons is, like that at New York's Grand Central, everything and there is no essential difference in character between Lyons-Satolas and Calatrava's airport terminal at Bilbao. In itself, this marks a reassertion of the dynamic, 'modern' image of the

railway, lost in recent years in the face of a general obsession with other modes of travel.

The context of Satolas is, of course, a large modern airport. Many current railway station projects are, in contrast, at the heart of established or developing urban areas where they may, indeed, be critical components. Foster's King's Cross terminal was seen as the key to the commercial redevelopment (largely as offices) of a 140-acre site, consisting of redundant railway sidings. Vittorio Gregotti's project for the recasting of the station quarter of Amadora (Portugal) addresses the problem which arises from the way in which railway's were allowed, in the past, to intrude ruthlessly into existing townscapes. At Amadora, which is a medium-sized town, the railway cut the community in two. Gregotti proposes a way in which the station can be commercially developed and the interests of the community served too. New public spaces sit on top of the tracks, giving access to the new buildings proposed as part of the development. Stirling Wilford's transport interchange for the Basque capital of Bilbao occupies a comparably pivotal position at the point where the ancient city meets its 19th-century commercial extension. It was at this point that the 19th-century railway engineers penetrated the city, laying down a swathe of tracks which cut Bilbao in two. Snaking across the valley, the railway and the city's main station were elevated on a substantial viaduct and embankment. Other transport facilities – including bus stations and the metro system – grew up piecemeal and poorly integrated with the main line terminus.

Stirling Wilford's strategy at Bilbao was to bring these facilities together in a development which is, typically for the practice, a defiantly pluralist urban statement – not so much a mega-structure as a collection of buildings, a city in miniature. The aim is to turn a great urban barrier into an urban focus by means of a new piazza, a roof garden and other public spaces. Housing, shops, offices and a new World Trade Centre are all integrated into the scheme. The primary identity of the complex, as a transport interchange, is indicated, however, by the looming presence of the great glass cube which allows entry to all levels. This is a dynamic feature: the symbol of a 'city of transportation' where the railway station is the most important part but is comprehended in a larger whole.

Similar motives underlie Terry Farrell's current transport schemes, most notably the new station for the Lantau and Airport Railway in Kowloon. The station is set in an intensive residential development – 4,000 apartments are located above it. The huge departure hall, however, emerges as a distinctive architectural feature and is top-lit. Farrell's proposed recasting of the

ABOVE: Alsop & Störmer's North Greenwich Station, Jubilee Line Extension; BELOW: Ian Ritchie Architects' Bermondsey Station, Jubilee Line Extension

Estacio do Rossio in Lisbon, in contrast, is a careful intervention into a classic 19th-century city terminus, Portugal's equivalent of St Pancras.

How far can there be a specifically late 20th-century approach to railway building? Several small to medium size British stations of recent vintage look specifically to the classic railway style of the past for inspiration. Troughton McAslan's Redhill station in Surrey pays homage, the architects concede, to Charles Holden's 'temple like' Arnos Grove on the Piccadilly Line, a 1930s classic, with its circular booking hall. This is seen as an urban symbol of the railway's presence – the station is a rebuilding of a nondescript 19th-century structure. The buildings at platform level are lightweight, even minimal – they are intended to be as functional as the trains. Architecture & Design Group has reworked the Arnos Grove formula for their recent station at North Woolwich, London. Alan Brookes Associates' East Croydon, one of the busiest stations in the London commuter belt, is a more expressive high-tech design. The form of the building derives from the requirement that it span across the tracks. The lightweight terminal sits on top, its roof supported on masts. The building fronts on to a small new square and provides an element of rational, humane design amidst the visual squalor of Croydon's office quarter. An equally positive urban gesture is provided by Kallmann, McKinnell, Wood's Back Bay station in Boston. The station (on the route from New York into Boston's South Station) had been closed many years ago and demolished. The site is close to Copley Square, with some of the city's most famous monuments, and to the bland mass of the 1980s Copley Place development in an area of civic and commercial importance. The reopening of the station was itself a significant move but the building is a triumph of rational transport design, quietly monumental but also open, spacious and reassuring, designed to lure back passengers to the railroad. America's traditional aversion to public transport has been increasingly challenged by the spread of green, environmentally aware thinking. In Los Angeles, the archetypal automobile city, a new metro system is under construction, reflecting a growing conviction that the car could eventually kill the city it effectively engendered. Architects Ellerbe Becket see the metro as 'a new typology for the metropolitan area'. Their Vermont/Santa Monica station 'affords an opportunity to address different urban forms and spatial experiences that have not existed before'. The 'subtle complexity' of the scheme (the architects' description) addresses both functional and urban issues, the latter specific to LA's idiosyncratic character. A highly expressive landmark is needed, both as a reference point for the traveller and as a symbol of the arrival of a novel transportation system.

The upgrading of the U5 Bahnhof line on the Berlin metro system has a similar significance for the newly reunited, but still highly disjointed, city. The line runs through what was East Berlin from Alexanderplatz and has been isolated from the remainder of the system. Integration – as well as improvement of passenger conditions – is the aim, contained in the brief for an international competition for the design of a prototype station. The competition was won by Richard Rogers Partnership last year. The Rogers proposal seeks to provide a linked sequence of spaces from street to train. At street level, curved glass shelters provide a landmark, a symbolic presence. The platform areas are naturally lit via skylights – the platforms (the architects say) will be 'sheltered street spaces by day and welcoming, glowing rooms by night'. Earlier mass transit systems – the London Underground, Paris Metro and New York Subway, for example – had been content to treat platform areas in a matter of fact way, accepting their subterranean nature. Increasingly, new systems seek to bring in natural lighting and reduce the threatening, enclosed character of stations.

Natural light is a feature of a number of stations on the new Jubilee Line in London, construction of which is scheduled for completion in 1996. The most spectacular of the stations, that by Norman Foster at Canary Wharf, will be entered through large glazed 'bubbles' which admit light to the booking hall and escalator bank. Ron Herron's Canada Water station will have a big, daylit ticket hall just below ground level. Ian Ritchie's Bermondsey station will have daylit platforms. The Jubilee Line, like the other major London rail project of the present day, Crossrail, represents a rejection of the philosophy of Frank Pick and Charles Holden – standardisation and a carefully controlled public image – in favour of a display of architectural virtuosity by a large number of practices. In part, this was the outcome of the need to get a large amount of design work done in a short time – no one practice could have designed the entire Jubilee Line in the allotted time – but it is equally a response to the varied, pluralistic architectural scene of eighties London. Uniformity of appearance is confined to the platforms.

The most spectacular of the Crossrail stations is that at Paddington, designed by Alsop & Störmer and to be built largely by means of a 'cut and cover' construction programme. Alsop makes impressive use of natural light, flooding it into the station through great slits at street level. Alsop is working with stained glass artist Brian Clarke on a programme of glazing to make maximum use of the opportunities to create a late 20th-century 'cathedral' of rail travel. Elsewhere on the route of Crossrail, station designs by (*inter alia*) Allies and Morrison, Michael Hopkins and Terry Farrell tackle the problem of integrating a major new rail network into the historic fabric of Westminster and the City of London.

The opposite approach – the imposition of a standard pattern of station design, providing instantly identifiable access points – has been pursued in most other new mass transit systems, for example, Norman Foster's new metro in Bilbao, scheduled to open late in 1995. With 36 stations and a track length of 60 kilometres, this is a large undertaking. The stations are identified by hood-shaped glass enclosures at ground level, as recognisable as the familiar rounder symbol of the London Underground.

These contrasting approaches illustrate the dilemma of public transport design today: ideals of transport as a public service conflict with an increasing pressure for consumer choice, and standardisation is at odds with local identity. In the late 20th century, as in the mid-19th century, the railway is seen as closely intertwined with the fate of whole communities. Then it was looked at as, on occasions, a destroyer. Now its influence is seen in more positive terms.

Just as mass transit railways relieve cities from the effects of ever-growing road traffic, so the high-speed intercity train is increasingly seen as an alternative to the crowded skies. The European TGV system has prompted major urban planning exercises in French cities like Lille, Tours and Nimes. A central element in the development of Berlin's Potsdamerplatz is a station on the line which links Moscow and Paris. Railways appear to have regained a role in the reshaping of continents.

Railways are big business. The French are hoping to export the TGV to California, Australia and China. They are also expensive to build and run. The international trend towards privatisation has seen Japan's State railway broken up, an impending privatisation of British Railways and moves in that direction in a number of European countries. (In the USA, passenger trains have been able to survive and revive only with the help of government money.) The contrast between a dynamic State enterprise and a faltering, half-privatised system is exemplified by the saga of the Channel Tunnel linking Britain and France. In Britain, the Waterloo Terminal has to be set against relatively mundane 'design and build' structures elsewhere on the route. A major out-of-London station planned for Ashford, Kent, has been much reduced in quality. A striking servicing shed designed by Ahrends, Burton & Koralek has been cancelled in favour of something altogether more utilitarian. But the worst, most notorious consequence of the refusal of the British government to invest substantially in the project is the fact that Paris-London trains will travel at 19th-century speeds between the Channel and Waterloo. In this light Nicholas Grimshaw's great shed on the South bank stands as an empty symbol of a new attitude to rail travel.

Sir Norman Foster & Partners' new passenger concourse building, King's Cross Station

CEZARY BEDNARSKI
HOMO ITINERANS

Life on Bucky Fuller's Spaceship Earth seems to be about travel and this not only by way of jetsetting around the Solar System and swirling with the Galaxy and the Universe. According to his sources, in 1800 an average adult walked some 1,100 miles per year and rode some ten miles. By 1900 it was still about 1,100 miles walked, but by then an average US citizen would have also ridden some 400 miles per year. In 1980 the average annual distance covered on foot surprisingly was still 1,100 miles but in the developed countries people averaged over 20,000 miles of vehicular travel. Before 1800 an average person would have covered only 30,000 miles in a lifetime.

There is no doubt that there is a growing need to cover more and more ground travelling. The present socio-economic system has brought with it the 'travel culture'. Growing material wealth combined with the growing volume of free time allows people to 'buy time'. Travel time is of great value in more than one way – be it travel for work or pleasure.

Cross border vehicular travel in the EC by EC citizens is estimated at 100 million journeys per year. Only 14 per cent of them are for business, a clear indication of the unstoppable developments in the field of telecommunications. According to a number of sources, within less than ten years tourism will become the single largest 'industry' on the globe. There is no leisure and tourism without transport, both local and long haul. If all of our travels, by whatever means, left trails like the condensation paths behind jet planes on the sky, seen from the moon the globe would seem entangled in a vast and quickly thickening cobweb of such vectors/trails produced by us in motion.

The second law of thermodynamics has been accepted as one of the basic laws in nature. It states that the natural flow of energy is from the state of greater differentiation and organisation to a state of lesser differentiation and organisation. At the bottom lies the state of ultimate disorganisation – the entropy. Paul K Feyerabend, the scientist branded 'the enemy of science' claims that 'there are no objective standards by which to establish truth' – a point of view popular with a great number of governments, although for less intellectual reasons. It would appear though that systems deprived of a supply of fresh energy and control do tend towards entropy. Transportation is such a system.

All modes of travel are interdependent. Unless techniques of transfer between modes and systems are radically improved even the most extraordinary improvements in the speed of a single means of transport or a system will not bring relevant improvement in time and efficiency of travel. More cars, more planes, more speed will continue to be defeated by an exponential increase in congestion and blockage of both systems and their interfaces. It is tunnel vision bringing with it waste of resources, discomfort, danger, social and environmental damage and entropy. Market forces are a one way street – a street of *more*. Transportation solutions have to be *designed* to take into account issues wider than just economics.

Homo Itinerans – maybe *Homo Urbanus*? According to the 1993 UN statistics the urbanisation index for Singapore is 100 per cent – hardly a surprise here, but it is 96 per cent for Belgium, 92 per cent for Israel, 91 per cent for Venezuela and 89 per cent for the UK. The world average is 44 per cent and between 1990 and 1995 world urbanisation will grow by 2.7-0.9 per cent in the developed areas and 3.7 per cent in those less developed – for example the urbanisation of Mozambique grows at 8.1 per cent and that of Afghanistan at 8.9 per cent. A global village or a global town Marshall McLuhan? There is no urban growth without transport, so in the light of the above statistics the issue of urban transport renders itself totally global and mammoth in scale.

Since the publication of TR Malthus' work *The Principle of Population* in 1798 it has been assumed by all political ideologies that there is a fundamental and grave inadequacy of life support on Earth. As a result poverty and hunger for vast millions of us has been accepted as unavoidable. This legacy has brought about paralysis in dealing with world scale problems, including the issue of travel. The prevailing economic status in the world is poverty. The gap between those with economic power and the rest of the global population is growing. At the same time travel has become both a social and economic necessity. The cost of travel has thus become a highly complex social, economic and environmental issue.

Traditionally, transportation infrastructure has been associated with enormous capital costs.

Governments and authorities habitually throw their people's tax money at solving transport issues, frequently in a very inefficient and inappropriate way, submitting to pressures from powerful self-centred lobbies. For example, the new road network on London's Isle of Dogs, with a land area just larger than Hyde Park, cost some £2.5 billion – nearly half the cost of the Channel Tunnel. It included 1.6 kilometres of Limehouse Link, a road which at £340 million (or £215.5 million per kilometre) was the most expensive ever built in the UK. The 12 kilometres of Dockland Light Railway, of dubious efficiency and logic, cost £800 million. Thirteen kilometres of the Lille metro in France, opened in 1982 and declared the most advanced metro in the world, cost £230 million. Was there no other option in Docklands? Who is going to pay for this? Of course there are other ways, and lessons can be learned from people who are not so well endowed with money and who cannot afford extravagance yet have the same needs. It takes only care and deeply understood responsibility on the part of decision makers.

The phenomenon of urbanisation is one of the most stunning inventions of our civilisation. Humanistic imagery would have cities as organisms with transport routes as their blood veins. But it is power that designs cities, not nature. Jaime Lerner, a Brazilian architect and planner, was quick to learn this simple lesson to the benefit of his city. He switched to politics and over the last 20 years served three terms as the mayor of Curitiba, the capital of the state of Parana in Brazil. His third term ended in 1991. Curitiba with a population of over 1.6 million – it was less that 500,000 in 1965 – is one of the fastest growing cities in Brazil. Its problems should grow at least as fast. Yet in 1990 Curitiba received the UN Environmental Programme Award for Achievement, nicknamed the 'Environmental Oscar'. Then came the International Institute for Energy Conservation Award for Achievement in Global Energetic Efficiency. In 30 years, thanks to political vision and consistency, Curitiba became an environmental city of global importance. Its Integrated Transportation Network is a key element of its social, economic and environmental success as a city.

Curitiba's planning process was initiated in 1964, after an open competition. Its implementation began in 1970. The plan follows a linear development concept along five transport spines channelling the structural growth of the city. The road network and public transport system have been most influential in sculpting the present shape of the city. It looks somewhat unusual with high buildings concentrated along the five routes. Faced with the all too well-known transport dilemma of private versus public, combined with the enormous costs of a solution recommended

by 'First World' transportation consultants involving an underground metro at $90-$100 million per kilometre and also favouring private cars on the ground, the city fathers had to think. The aim was in principle relatively simple – to transport more people at a lesser cost, giving priority to collective transport over that of the individual. With full appreciation of the social importance of transportation, Curitiba discarded the idea of an underground as well as, at $20 million per kilometre, the cheaper option of a light rail system, and set out to design its own solution. The Curitiba Direct Route Busway System, with elegantly simple and logical 'tube stops' was built at a cost of $0.2 million per kilometre. The Curitiba Integrated Transit Network was established in 1980. It did not require tunnels, bridges, underpasses, multi-level junctions or other capital guzzling civil engineering structures. There is a less perfect world elsewhere. The elevated freeways of California were the most explicit victims of the recent earthquakes. Car based transportation suffered dramatically and degenerated into chaos. Now the USA faces a bill of billions of dollars to rebuild what cost billions to build in the first place. 'If we seek merely swollen, slothful ease then bolder and stronger peoples will pass us by', Theodore Roosevelt once said.

Curitiba zoning was subordinated to the transport network. As a result it was possible not only to locate places of work close to transport routes but also high density housing. Some 17,000 lower income families, traditional users of public transport, live in close proximity to the network. Although a relatively prosperous city by Brazilian standards, about 10 per cent of the population of Curitiba continues to live in *favelas* – squatter settlements on the outskirts of the city. These people cannot afford cars and have to rely on public transport if they are to participate in the social and economic life of the city. In most Brazilian *favelas* there is no refuse collection, mainly because of lack of access roads. Their poor reputation is closely linked to dirt and litter. A very successful scheme encouraged *favela* residents in Curitiba to collect and sort their refuse which is then bought by the city in return for bus tickets and fresh food. The programme has led to a considerable decrease in city pollution, and has improved sanitation and health standards as well as the quality of life for the urban poor. It has allowed them to rejoin society and has reduced the risk of a Los Angeles style social uprising. Income earned by the city from selling recyclable garbage is reinvested in the city's social programmes.

Car ownership in Curitiba is much higher than in other major Brazilian cities. Although there are well over 500,000 cars in the city, Curitiba does not have traffic problems and the average traffic

Embarkation/disembarkation at a 'tube stop', Curitiba Direct Route Busway System, Brazil

speed of over 20 kilometres per hour is higher than that in most cities of a comparable size. Curitiba's public transportation system is used by more than 1.3 million passengers a day and attracts nearly two-thirds of the city's population (28 per cent of the Direct Line 'Speedy' bus users previously travelled by car). The switch to public transport has helped to reduce city-wide fuel consumption by some 25 per cent. Each of the recently introduced bi-articulated buses replaces three conventional size buses thus reducing exhaust emissions per passenger by almost two-thirds. In the last two years, half the city fleet of buses has been replaced with vehicles propelled by turbo engines, allowing a further 50 per cent reduction in emission levels compared with normally aspirated engines. Curitiba has one of the lowest rates of air pollution in Brazil and this can be attributed directly to the reduced use of cars. According to research at Columbia University cars use 1,860 calories per passenger per mile, buses 920, rail 885, walking 100 and cycling only 35. In 1992 Curitiba had 153 kilometres of cycle routes.

The success of Curitiba's bus system is partially due to the 'trinary road system' which is formed by a central street with a separate two way lane for buses in the middle flanked by two one way slow traffic lanes. In order to avoid 60-metre-wide roads, one block behind, on either side, there is a one-way fast traffic street parallel to the central street. Public transport, building density and road hierarchy are covered in one planning guideline.

Unexpected failures in systems stem from component failure and these arise from material flows. But systems can be designed to work even when their parts fail – the key is redundancy. It can provide an exponential growth of a system's reliability. A more powerful form of redundancy is design diversity – systems with different designs working in parallel. System expansion based on analysis of its performance allows evolutionary development along a critical path. Curitiba's transportation system is based on an evolutionary approach related to the growth of the city and its population. It is managed by URBS (Urbanisation of Curitiba), a mixed capital company, and is being constantly developed and tuned by the Curitiba Research and Urban Planning Institute (IPPUC), a true laboratory of ideas which changed the fate of the city.

In the cities of countries like Brazil, with sudden and dramatic demographic growth, saturation of transport systems is a constant threat. The Integrated Transportation Network fully coped with the growing needs for a number of years eventually reaching a peak of some 15,000 people per hour in one direction. This was quite a performance for a bus network. The continuing development of Curitiba along the north/south axis led to saturation. In 1990 the 'Speedy' Direct

Lines were introduced to cope. They run in parallel with the existing axis but have less frequent stops and a new fare configuration.

The latest innovation is the design of the Direct Line stops. Transportation systems are as efficient as the speed at which they can load and unload passengers and return to their maximum velocity. Rather than increase the number of buses the Curitiba designers looked carefully at the issue of boarding them. The result was a 'tube stop' which offers the same speed, safety and comfort of loading and disembarking as an underground train. The tube stops are elevated boarding platforms with their floor level at the same height as the bus floor, where passengers pay before boarding. The facility is four times faster than traditional street level stops allowing up to eight passengers a second to board, which dramatically increases the number of passengers carried by a given number of buses. Made of steel and eight-millimetre laminated glass they have entrance and exit turnstiles and a ticket selling position. Each stop is 10 metres long and weighs five tonnes. The closing and opening of the tube and bus pneumatic doors is controlled by an infrared sensor with a transmitter on the bus. According to the World Health Organisation one could expect some 80,000 disabled people in a city the size of Curitiba. Each of the tube stations is fitted with a disabled hoist. The ability to use standard transport facilities enables disabled people to rejoin the full life of the city without feeling like special outsiders. This is more than can be said for practically any other city I know, where to get onto public transport one has to climb or descend stairs. In Curitiba wheelchair users do not pay for public transport, and to complement the bus service, the disabled can be picked up from home and delivered to a stop by special vans operated by URBS.

All of Curitiba's Integrated Transit System is a joint venture between the city and the private sector. The buses are privately owned by companies with concessions to operate specific routes. The government sets out guidelines and monitors the performance of the system. Bus fares go to a municipal bus fund managed by the URBS and the private bus companies are paid in accordance with the distance that their buses cover in service. The whole system operates without any direct subsidies. Private investment in the Direct Line 'Speedy' Network was $45 million with a contribution from the city of US $4.5 million. An electric tram line, as an alternative, was estimated to cost US $240 million. Common sense and care prevailed again.

In 1992 Curitiba introduced the bi-articulated bus as the most logical solution to the dawning crisis of system capacity saturation. Faced with

ABOVE: Direct Line 'Speedy' bi-articulated bus; BELOW: 'Tube stop', an elevated boarding platform with its floor level the same height as the bus floor

its own meagre financial resources and the all Brazilian difficulty in securing foreign money brought about by the dubious assistance from the international banking system, Curitiba yet again had to be creative. The bi-articulated bus was designed in Brazil with assistance from Volvo in Sweden. The starting premise was that maybe more could be squeezed out of buses in terms of capacity. With the bi-articulated bus measuring 25 metres in length and capable of carrying 270 passengers and boarding through the tube stops, the capacity of up to 22,000 passengers per hour in one direction was achieved. A light railway system at a much higher capital cost would be hard pushed to get anywhere near this figure. It is more like the capacity of an underground system. In operation they offer a 12.5 per cent reduction in cost if compared with standard buses. The bi-articulated buses are the 'running stock' of the fully blown Curitiba 'surface subway' which opened in December 1992 on the Boqueirao route. The current rush hour peak one way flow is approximately 10,000 passengers. In total 130,000 people use the route daily travelling with an average speed approaching 30 kilometres per hour – some sort of record for urban traffic speed. On average these people save one hour per day on their travel time, have more private time, less stress, work better and are more relaxed at home. How can this be measured and summarised statistically?

But this is not the end of Curitiba's ambitions. Development strategies must involve people, *principia* and institutions but they must also rest on tactics which inevitably involve technology. The next step in Curitiba is the installation of on-board computers which will control passenger flow and time scheduling. The whole URBS fleet will be constantly finely tuned by computer programmes. In a matter of minutes any element of the system will be adjusted to meet varying passenger demands as registered throughout the day. This will prevent both losses resulting from vehicles running below their capacity and passenger discomfort caused by overloading. The current network is also being expanded to include regional transport. Personally, I will be disappointed if within a relatively short time we do not hear from Curitiba again with a new scheme involving say the use of Photovoltaic (PV) generated electricity to power lightweight carbon fibre bodied buses gliding on diamond coated friction free bearings. They may even be powered by flywheel kinetic energy storage systems with continuous transmission gearboxes. After all, in 1975 Brazil set up the world's biggest experiment in alternative fuel: the Proalcohol programme. There is so much talk about energy saving these days. Yet all the energy we use at present represents less than some 1/10,000 of the solar energy reaching the Earth. 'We worry not about energy

but about convenient supplies of gas and oil', said Eric Drexler in his *Engines of Creation*. An urban transportation network run on electricity generated by PV panels used in place of expensive, high quality building cladding panels and routed via the state grid is feasible. It cannot be that far off. It simply makes sense and there is so much sun in Brazil. 'He that will not apply new remedies must expect new evils for time is the greatest innovator', said Francis Bacon over 300 years ago.

In May 1991 an experimental line of the 'Speedy' bus was set up in the southern end of Manhattan. *Chapeau bas*! to the courage of the New York City municipality. It involved four stepless buses and four 'tube stops'. Over 80,000 New Yorkers were able to sample the elegance of thought and efficiency of the system. They all saved 50 per cent of their travel time as compared with the normal New York City bus network.

The Curitiba example clearly shows that the way in which we travel and transport our goods has to be constantly reviewed. The environmental, social and economic performance of means, systems and interfaces have to be monitored and adjusted at local, regional and international level.

The International Civil Aviation Organisation is concerned that the current volume of 700 aircraft daily crossing the Atlantic will double by the year 2010. Separation zones between planes in flight are to be reduced to allow more planes into the air. The issue of concern is human safety. Yet already the current volume of traffic causes vapour trail clouds shading the North Atlantic. Significant reductions in the growth of plankton and fish stock have been observed. Scientists now talk not only about the 'ozone hole' but also the 'green algae hole'. Green algae need sun for photosynthesis and are believed to be the key climate stabilizers on a global scale. In addition to being environmentally damaging, air travel is not efficient in terms of use of time and energy. I need six hours to get from Central London to the centre of Warsaw 1571 kilometres away. The flight takes 2.5 hours but my average speed is 261 kilometres per hour. Even if the plane travelled at 1,500 kilometres per hour I would still need 4.5 hours – an average speed of 349 kilometres per hour. Getting to and from airports increases my travel cost by 25 per cent.

TGV Atlantique in France achieves a maximum speed of 300 kilometres per hour. Yoshihiro Kyotani's MAGLEV train holds the world train speed record of 517 kilometres per hour. The 300X series Shinkansen train in Japan will soon travel at a commercial speed of 350 kilometres per hour. In Europe there is already clear evidence that high-speed rail attracts passengers who previously travelled by road and air. By the

ABOVE: 'Tube stop' showing entrance and exit turnstiles; BELOW: Each station is fitted with a disabled hoist

year 2010 the expanded high-speed European rail network will reach 286 billion passenger kilometres. Seventy-three per cent of passenger volume increase will be travellers 'poached' from roads and air. At present fast rail service is particularly competitive with air travel on journeys of up to three hours. In 1992 TGV Sud-Est achieved an 80 per cent average load factor – a dream rate for airlines. Railways beat air travel on cost and convenience. The speed of travel is where they seem to be losing, particularly on long distances – or are they?

At a 1978 meeting of the American Association for the Advancement of Science, Robert M Salter of RAND Corporation presented the concept of a global underground – appropriate enough, considering the urbanisation of the Earth. The idea of Planetran was conceived over 20 years ago. The fastest option examined was a US coast-to-coast journey of 21 minutes (a plane needs 20 minutes just to reach its cruising altitude . . .), achieving 1g propulsion and a maximum speed of 22,500 kilometres per hour. Travelling from the centre of New York to the centre of Los Angeles the carriages are constantly accelerated to the midpoint and from there constantly decelerated. Extensive research would need to be carried out to determine passenger responses to such acceleration. An option easier on the imagination was a 54 minute journey at a maximum speed of 9,600 kilometres per hour.

Electromagnetically suspended and propelled Planetran carriages would travel along evacuated underground tubes which can link all the continents. The only undersea crossings required would be the Bering Straits and the South East Asian Islands on the way to Australia. It would interface with all the existing transport systems and would offer a low-cost, safe, convenient, efficient and non-polluting alternative to air travel.

Tunnelling is the major cost of the system. This element was most frequently attacked as not feasible by its opponents, who by and large had vested interest in other modes of long distance travel. Tunnelling, however, is a well known area of engineering expertise, the most notable recent example being the Channel Tunnel, larger in diameter than that required for the Planetran. Thousands of kilometres of tunnels are drilled in the world every year. In the sixties it was some 13,000 kilometres in the Western countries alone. The adversaries of the concept were not willing to accept that the cost of Planetran tunnels as infrastructure should be looked at in the context of the infrastructure required to get people on board planes and get the planes into the air – these costs are comparable. Using superconductors, magnetic levitation and propulsion in 1 per cent sea level air pressure allows a 98 per cent energy efficiency for Planetran travel – the New York to Los Angeles travel would cost $1.00 per

passenger in energy costs. RM Salter estimated that the incredible energy efficiency of the system and its minimal environmental impact would make it possible to recover the cost of tunnelling within one year just through savings in energy use.

Planetran does not require any scientific or technological breakthrough, we could get on with it right now. What is required is a thinking breakthrough and sustained political consistency as shown in Curitiba over the last 25 years. For the moment the 'run-away' air travel goes on. Apparently Boeing and Airbus would have had full order books were it not for the current recession. Predictions say that air travel will grow annually by about 5.2 per cent until the year 2010. Billions of pounds worth of new planes, airports and infrastructure will be built worldwide. There is a lively political tradition that fosters suspicion of technology. The oldest and most effective mental immune response is simply to believe the old and reject the new. To quote E Drexler: 'Sloth, intellectual, moral and physical seems perhaps the greatest danger. We can only meet great challenges with great effort. Will enough people make enough effort? Success will require only that a growing community of people strives to develop, publicise and implement workable solutions. But passionate concern and action will not be enough; we will also need sound policies.'

The 'mad plane' disease is spreading and so is the 'mad car' affliction. At present both are heading towards entropy. To park the current population of the world cars an area larger than Wales, or most of Lebanon, is used every day. They need much more space when in motion. Statistically nearly one-third of land in cities is devoted to cars. Daniel Goeudevert of Volkswagen says: ' People who saw streets and multistorey car parks harvest traffic jams'. It has been estimated that in the West Midlands the annual cost of traffic congestions is £600 million in lost time and resources, this sum does not include long term environmental losses. In 1984, four per cent of the total annual petrol consumption in the USA was burned up in traffic jams. The newly 'capitalised' Eastern and Central Europe is quickly catching up. Thirty per cent of traffic in central Budapest is caused by drivers looking for parking spaces. In Warsaw cars are parked on pavements and lawns. The car is the new icon, an attribute of the state of personal freedom and independence. One has to have a toothbrush, shoes and a car, or is the order different? As Colin Cherry wrote in 1966: 'People driving cars don't form a society in any sense. There is no doubt that driving produces a change of personality'. Great Britain is near the top of the European charts on the number of pedestrian deaths in road

ABOVE: TGV Atlantique, France; BELOW: Cars parked on the pavement, Warsaw

accidents. There are 4,000 deaths on British roads every year – the equivalent of ten Jumbo Jets crashing down on the island. The British roads have become lethal for children, more than a third of all road accidents involve walking children. In 1971, 80 per cent of children went to school on their own, in 1993 only nine per cent are allowed to do so by their parents.

There is no doubt that cars are useful. They are most efficient for areas of random movement. Comfort, convenience, privacy, storage, guaranteed seating and independence from timetables in addition to a number of intangible satisfactions make the use of car attractive. The car manufacturers are fighting back. They recognise that unless the current 'car problem' can be resolved there will be no cars in the future.

There are a number of issues to resolve. First of all is the issue of pollution including the recently publicised lethal microscopic particles. In addition to ever cleaner and more efficient internal combustion engines new forms of propulsion are being developed including electric, kinetic, hydrogen and hybrid. Annual expenditure on developing electric vehicles exceeds five billion pounds worldwide. All major car manufacturers are testing electric cars. All have a problem with the energy storage capacity of batteries and their cost – the BMW E1 sodium sulphur battery costs £16,000. Interestingly, nobody seems to have suggested that batteries rather than being bought with cars remain the property of their manufacturers. One would drive up to a 'battery station' and swap a flat battery for a loaded one, paying just for charging and depreciation.

The AFS20 car developed in the USA is to be powered by kinetic energy stored in a high speed flywheel spinning in a vacuum at 200,000 rpm. This is a very high tech version of the principle used in Parry People Mover trams made in the UK. Tapping 'Zero Point Energy', Stanley A Meyer of Ohio seems close to presenting a working vehicle powered by hydrogen derived from water. He estimates that a conversion kit for a petrol engine, once in production, would cost some $1,500. Weight for weight, hydrogen has about 2.5 times the explosive power of petrol. The process of 'hydrogen fracturing' offers virtually instantaneous generation of hydrogen without the

need to store it, thus the system should be entirely safe. This fascinating possibility has been recently summarised by Admiral Sir Anthony Griffin in his paper 'Energy from Water'. Amory Lovins of the Rocky Mountain Institute, the advocate of a hybrid supercar capable of 300 mpg said: 'Modern cars are an extraordinary engineering achievement but like many technologies they have reached their peak of sophistication, they have become fundamentally obsolete.'

The next issue is the size of cars, particularly for town driving where space is so valuable. At present in the UK the owner of a Fiat Cinquecento (3.22 x 1.48 metres = 4.76 square metres) and the owner of a Bentley (5.3 x 1.9 metres = 10.07 square metres) pay the same amount of road tax and the same parking charges. This is insane. It is quite telling that over the last ten years or so cars have been getting smaller in size. I think that the optimum would be a very small car (of say some 1.5 x 2.5 metres in plan), two of which could be parked on a parking meter. Such cars could be rented as and when needed from a corner car rental point where they would be stored vertically on racks. Most of urban travel would be using cheap and efficient public transport, and long distance travel would be by high speed collective transport with small car rental points at all stations. One would never need to own a car. The nano-technologist Eric Drexler said: 'Genuine courage requires facing reality, facing accelerating change in a world that has no automatic brakes. This poses intellectual, moral and political challenges of great substance . . . Our machines are evolving faster than we [are]. Unless we learn to live with them safely, our future will likely be both exciting and short.'

Then, there still is the possibility of walking . . . But following Jane Austen's advice: 'Let other pens dwell on guilt and misery'. Humanity is at the centre of the universe and time and space are there for us to travel through. The issue is by what means?

Homo Viator
(Medieval concept of human condition – the wandering man).

The different shape, dimension and type of vehicles

TRAVELLING ARCHITECTS

VAN BERKEL & BOS
Das Schloss – A Reconstruction of
Change

The airport, railway station, underground;
the tunnel, bridge, highway cross-over:
these represent the key places of contemporary urban life. Public and intermediate,
each leads the double life of all extensive
urban and infrastructural objects; for
despite their sometimes massive architectural solidity, in the individual, subjec-
tive experience they are short-lived,
intensive and divided. The two realities
exist concurrently, a bridge being there as
a fixed point in the city and also as a
fragmented series of images of stays,
lights, traffic lanes. The multiple identity is
insurmountable at every level. However
one approaches the project, ambiguities,
transformations and combinations of
forces keep clamouring to the fore.

This was our experience while working
on a number of such intermediate objects,
most notably the Erasmus bridge in
Rotterdam which will be completed at the
end of 1995. To attribute such manifest
asymmetry to an urban project is probably
the bridge's most provocative aspect. It is
impossible to simply reduce the urban
effect of the bridge to that of landmark, for
it stems from an extensive programme at
various scales of planning to which no
single architectural gesture is applicable.

The quality of mobility, stemming from
and concurring with the bridge's identity
as a place of 'transport interchange',
expresses itself as a form of transgres-
sion. It is the result of different fields of
forces impinging upon another. Interpretations of what these forces constitute are
not seen as stable categories, but are
subject to change. Just as in the blink of
an eye the point of focus changes and
alters perception, bringing some objects
nearer while rendering others vague, the
public and physiological forces of architecture are always in motion; they are
never distinct, severable, static.

For this reason, the 'laws' the architect
comes across in the fields of the laws of
nature, urban expectations and engineering, which are the different levels of
reality with which he engages himself,
float like objects between stations where
projects such as these are concerned. On
each level everything moves; the balance
between substance and process,
materiality and transport is at the core of
the architecture of interchange.

Adapted from 'Mobile Forces' by Ben van
Berkel and Caroline Bos, from the new
monograph on the work of Ben van Berkel
entitled Crossing Points, published in Autumn
1994 by Ernst & Sohn, Berlin.

IAN RITCHIE
Termini

In my mind, transport interchanges are seldom places which celebrate arrival or departure, which for many, remain the domain of the transport terminus. The terminus is a Victorian word associated with railways, whereas the terminal is a 20th-century word associated with airports and the world of electronics. Both, of course, only exist because of the other end.

Of course, in today's commuter world, many termini and terminals now function as interchanges to be negotiated at speed. Travel time is a significant factor in determining one's emotional condition prior to encountering an interchange, a term I would use to describe all ports of call in any journey I make. Generally, those journeys with a long travel time or where much time has passed before returning home, open up the possibility to experience a sense of departure and/or arrival, and where the architecture of the interchange can affect me. Perhaps, because I travel so much around Europe on short business trips, and no major interchange is accessible from my office or home without using either the London Underground or a taxi, mentally, the experience of departure is conditioned by the impending assault course. Even the major interchange is not a place to tarry, but to be negotiated as fast as possible, to avoid the ubiquitous retailing opportunity with its material and visual paraphernalia.

I find that I can appreciate the architecture of transport interchanges when coming in to land and seeing the interchange in the context of the city, or when there is a delay in the scheduled travel arrangements, which of course then changes my emotional state of mind! In the case of the latter, this has a more negative effect when I am on the return journey than when I am outward bound, since I am usually looking forward to getting home. In these circumstances one is usually somewhere on the periphery of the interchange, in an air conditioned transit lounge with its en suite self-service coffee trolley and maybe Duty Free outlet. Here, the quality of the external view to obtain a sense of the outside climate (and the information update) becomes most important.

In general, I feel, railway interchanges remain far better environments than airports, probably because one can usually choose to be in the outside climate, appreciate the transport vehicles, the metal carpet zig-zagging off to the horizon and appreciate the overall architecturally engineered space. Railway interchanges are also a strategic and visually important part of the central and public urban fabric which airports can never be until there is a major technical evolution of the craft. Maybe airports should always have outside terraces, adjacent to departure gates, rather than just the regimented rows of international seats and uniform lighting in sanitised environments and where food and retail structures block views.

I never travel with baggage, which allows me, quite often, to switch planes or the mode of travel, reducing the amount of time I have to spend in them. Today the strongest impression I have is that most major interchanges are now designed to make more money from retailing and advertising than they do from their 'primary' function.

29

LEBBEUS WOODS
Stranger

The airport again. Movement and anonymity. Suspension of time, of purposes, of histories. The utter strangeness of a self-imposed exile between arrivals and departures. A few hours of being no place at all. Knowledge without interest, Schopenhauer called it, knowledge disconnected from desiring, from any particular purpose and meaning. Nothing to do but wait. Nothing to do but think. Nothing to do but draw. But to do, think and draw . . . what? The project left behind, or waiting ahead? That's only an escape from the quiet terror of this freedom, a way of negating its feelings of loss, of pretending that one has never left home, or has already arrived there.

Others, anonymous comrades in these hours of exquisite awkwardness, are shopping in the duty-free zone, or are sitting with a book, trying to overcome the discomfort of being nowhere. They aren't really here, won't remember this place, won't tell their friends and families about it. They won't understand that they've always been here, have always been strangers, will always be strangers, wherever they go, whomever they are with. Then they will be strangers to themselves. But who, then, will they be?

Better to be always in-between, to have no absolute points of reference, to watch the monitors displaying the departures of flights, to know that your flight will depart more or less on time and that you must be on it, that it is the lifeline to some meaning you've invested your life in, that everything is riding on your being on that airplane, and yet to play, seriously, with the thought that you may not be. This play liberates, because it makes clear the choices you make, not just here, but everywhere. Everything is choice. Nothing is given as certain, already concluded. Determinism is not determined, after all, but is only a choice. Things are moving,

and the pattern of their movements must be chosen from among many possible patterns at a given moment, during the hours of uncertainty and suspension. When you measure light for the properties of a particle, it behaves like a particle; when you measure for a wave, it behaves like a wave. The act of observation is part of the phenomena observed. You are not only part of the flow, you are the flow. The flow is manifest only through you, your perception, your invention. But only if you see it, and then, only if you act . . . if you flow, too. If you measure the moment for the properties of time and space, it behaves like architecture. Architecture is an action and a choosing. It is a flow of choices by the architect, liberating the possibility of possibilities for others. In the airport, this is always most clear.

WILLIAM ALSOP
Transport Interchanges

These are places that have become increasingly a part of my life. As mobility increases through both desire and necessity they will become a normal part of everyone's lives. When movement was special, the art of arrival and departure was too. People would dress up to fly on aeroplanes, or conducted great celebrations on the disembarkation of a great ship. Many transport interchanges, like the bus stations in New York, have become gathering places for itinerant migrants who find security in others' brief experiences of travelling. Places of travel now offer large, well serviced roofs to the needy. They provide places for the homeless to become anonymous within a crowd. They give hope to people who believe that great mechanical bents, whether plane, train, bus or ship can transport them to better lives with less problems. The social side of these places should not be reduced by the idea of good design.

Today I do not believe that I still have to wait at airports, ferry terminals or train stations. I do not believe how pathetic my air ticket is, and how easy it is to discard it together with the rest of the extraneous pieces of paper you require to allow you to move from one place on the earth's surface to another. I cannot believe that you cannot lay down on an aeroplane and sleep.

The transport industry and its associated buildings require major shift in thinking if society is to tolerate them in future.

I would like to get on and off various modes of transport where I want to. I propose a greater number of smaller dispersed airports. I demand a service. I demand greater democracy in terms of numbers of geographical locations served.

Rome Termini is generous enough to give the user three different large spaces to transverse between the train and the taxi. These spaces are much larger than required but they allow the traveller the opportunity to make the transition from the confines of a rail compartment to a city with both style and dignity. I am not sure that the airport style departure lounges at Waterloo station will do the same job. I am not there for convenience of the station management, I wish to enjoy the fact that I have to move. Some interchanges that ought to exist don't. For example bike to bus, car to train, plane to bike, or indeed plane to foot.

Why should a supermarket not be an interchange between bus, food and taxi? Why should trains not be offices with waiting rooms and proper communications systems? Why can't I get a haircut on a train? etc, etc. . .

Time spent travelling and changing from one mode of transport to another is my time – my life. It should contribute to all that is good and not be seen, as it is all to often a necessary bind.

Stevenson said that it is better to travel than to arrive. Today he might have said it is better not to travel at all.

SHIN TAKAMATSU
Transport Interchanges

In general, the concept of transportation tends to be described physically in terms of buses, aeroplanes or trains. However, if one assumes that traffic is the interaction of different cultures, information or languages, then it means the concept of internationalisation described by Marx.

Transport Interchanges are the places where people exchange their culture, language or information for their own development, or it is the place where different ideas meet. As an architect, I believe the most important factor is to provide more open space for traffic, in other words, to be able to structure space to produce a difference in culture, language and value, and thus, activate the traffic.

Currently in progress, the Nagasaki Ferry Terminal is a passenger terminal, serving a ferry sailing between Nagasaki city and neighbouring islands. The programme is not as simple as it seems because it requires complicated functions, almost like an international airport, for every island possesses its own culture. The concept is clear and simple; to develop space as a vessel which activates the traffic, for the communication between people.

In the Shichiruiko Terminal Plan, boats sail only between Shichiruiko and Okinoshima island so that the function is limited compared with Nagasaki. Our architectural intention here is to build a gate for passengers and a machine to produce more traffic. This terminal also contains public space for interaction between passengers and city residents.

Future Port City has the image of a near-futuristic high-tech airport. This is a proposal for the environment or for a nation which is the symbol of interaction among race, nation and culture rather than as a transportation facility. The three projects differ from each other in concept, but share the similar idea of interaction of people, language and culture.

STUDIO ASYMPTOTE

New York departure 2100 hours, Paris arrival 0900 hrs

The airport signifies neither gate nor portal, rather it is a realm of anticipatory trajectories structured on desire and displacement. All destinations whether to a neighbouring city or the edge of some far-off continent are equalised and seemingly inconsequential. What does matter is punctuality, personal identification and procedure. The waiting areas all resemble one another despite the diverse accumulation of people that linger oblivious to their impending state of purgatory. Airport space is city space, filled to capacity with the vectors of urban life; a space where a strange sort of social democracy prevails and where no one seems unnecessarily concerned with their own equalised state and levelled status. The airport is always located at the margin of some city, well outside its limits and reality. The brief and transient moments experienced in an airport terminal are only offset by the deafening din of anonymity that fills these spaces. Even the fuselage of the plane transforms into a seemingly infinitely extruded waiting area where physical mobility is eradicated and supplanted by a fixed and prolonged disembodiment. The video monitors centrally placed for optimum viewing at various points within the tubular interior reveal an array of real time information that unfolds otherwise invisible experiences: the current altitude, exterior air temperature, ground speed and the aircraft's precise location at any given moment. This flickering computer simulation appears just prior to take-off, lending an air of comfort and familiarity while feigning a sense of place in this otherwise placeless environment. Once airborne a laptop computer is activated, a hypertext document flashes on the LCD screen moving as a dense liquid from one array to the next, revealing at times a drawing, images then text, an incongru-ous collection of information that seems incomprehensible to your neighbour. The inflight movie stammers onto the video screens drawing all activity in the cabin to a halt as each passenger attaches himself to a headset, surrendering to Hollywood manufactured images of consensus. The flight attendant requests that window shades be lowered to optimise viewing of the film; those wishing to view the clouds and oceans passing by at 500 mph do so with a sense of guilt and subversion. An attendant's peddling of duty-free goods or the pilot's innocuous reporting of land-marks below interrupt the serene eupho-ria of this drive-through space and multiple time zones. The illumination of the fasten seat belt signs is followed by an abrupt jolt mark, the inevitability of landing in yet another interstitial zone of transience. The arrival gates differ slightly from those designated for departure left some 4,000 miles behind. Here, minute signs of difference found mainly in postcards, momentos and other para-phernalia are displayed within spaces of delirium and commerce. A carefully delineated post-modernist agglomeration of distilled events and constructed perfection makes apparent the strange simulcra of the city, its infrastructure, architecture and inhabitants imparted upon travellers meandering through these hygienic bazaars. Seamlessly linked to all other air-ports (cities) through the archaic implement of air flight, the air terminal of today is a condensed spatial apparatus which mimics the city and aspires to be a cybernetic circumstance.

To travel today is to partake in an experience of urban distillation, a space of endless distractions and distortion rivalled only by telephone and television inter-activity. Notions of visiting, compre-hending and remembering are displaced and perhaps even re-invigorated in such a redefined spatiality. Amidst these awk-ward, yet vital, frames of indifference and simulation another architecture thrives.

WILLIAM ALSOP
HAMBURG FERRY AND CRUISE SHIP TERMINAL
Germany

When Phase 3 is completed the terminal will be 500 metres long, the longest office building in Europe, maximising and epitomising the city's longstanding affinity with the River Elbe and its connection to the sea. The creation of a building to reflect this relationship was the key consideration in the design and development of the project. The water side of the building is visually open to and embraces the river and shipping, while the land side is less so. The green glass walls overlooking the river reflect the colour and patterns of the water, while the silver metal spandrel panels present a more solid face to the street. The exception is at the ground floor where a double-height glass wall allows the visitor a clear view through the public areas to the water and ships beyond. There is a car parking area under the cruise terminal (Phase 2) creating the effect of a moat spanned by bridges which give visitors access to that part of the building. The floors above are for administration and office functions. The concrete 'A' shaped structural columns are reminiscent of the cranes and derricks along the quayside, but it is in the materials and details of the structure, such as the support for the viewing balcony, and other building elements like the automatically adjustable sun visors, that the maritime feeling is really captured – though never allowed to become a pastiche.

This building gave us the opportunity to build by the water. What a piece of water! The Elbe flows with life and creates new images continuously. Sometimes it becomes aggressive and floods to new proportions (approximately six times a year). Our building facilitates views of this mighty river from a safe haven. I know from having an office adjacent to the Thames, that continual views of water are not always welcome, particularly on melancholic February mornings. This can be overcome by concentrating on the quality of light in the building. There needs to be a subtle combination of lightness and cosiness. The building has eyelids on the south side. Sometimes it is necessary to close one's eyes to the external world. The building blinks as it creates an edge to help channel the Elbe. Every street needs an edge definition and in this respect the Elbe is no exception. Our street edge offers a line of parallel platforms from which to both observe and hide from the River. William Alsop

BELOW: Roof plan; OVERLEAF, FAR RIGHT: Cross sections

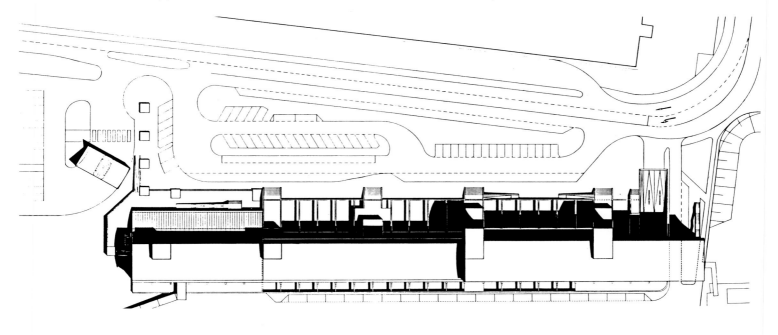

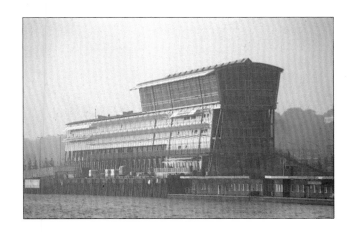

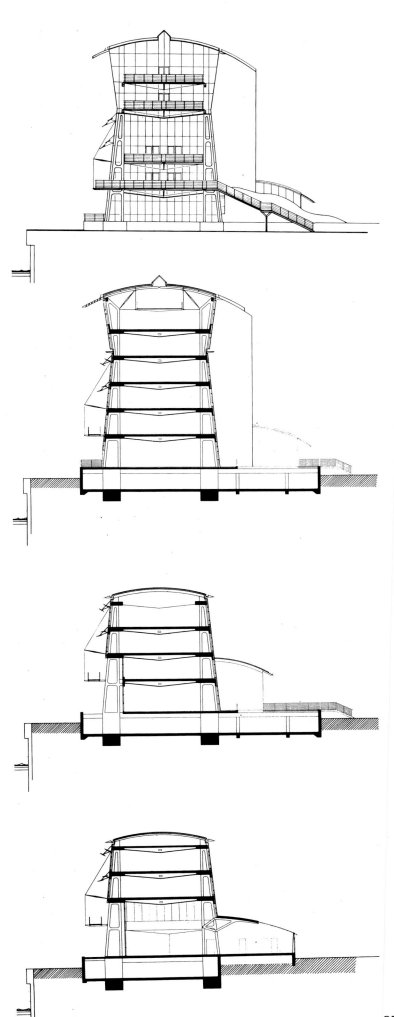

ELLERBE BECKET

VERMONT/SANTA MONICA METRO RED-LINE STATION
Los Angeles

The Vermont/Santa Monica Station is part of a plan intended to improve the connections between Los Angeles neighbourhoods with rapid transit trains. It comprises the intersection of Vermont Avenue and Santa Monica Boulevard in Hollywood.

Ellerbe Becket is providing architectural design services for this project which consists of a public plaza on Vermont Avenue, a 450-foot long underground station and a circulation area which connects the two spaces. A stainless steel canopy, cantilevered 30 feet above the plaza, signals the entrance to the station.

For Los Angeles, the construction of the Metro Rail constitutes a new typology for the metropolitan area. This urban intervention affords an opportunity to address different urban forms and spatial experiences that have not existed before. This project attempts to understand and define some of these issues and to approach a solution of subtle complexity. One of the largest stations on the Red Line, running from downtown Angeles to North Hollywood, Vermont/Santa Monica is located one block from the Braille Institute and is adjacent to Los Angeles City College. Due to its proximity to these institutions, the project incorporates in its design the art programmes of the college and utilises architectural elements of light, sound and materials to aid visually-impaired users.

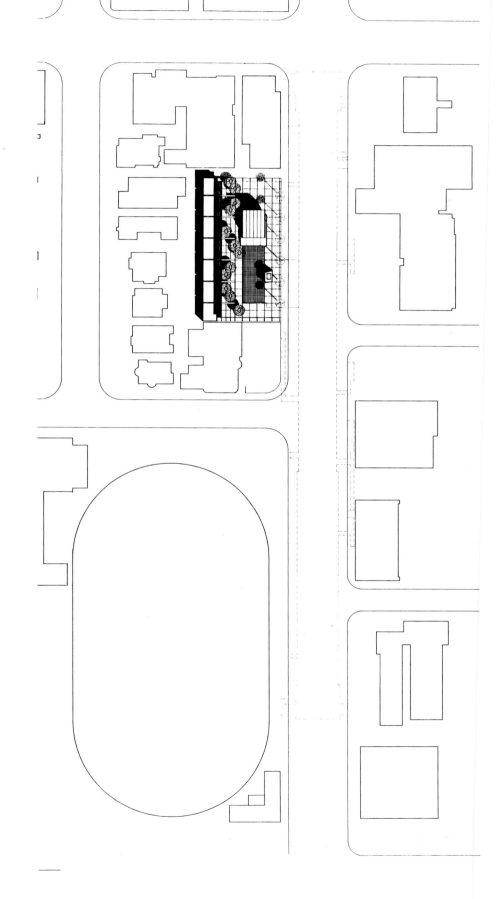

RIGHT: Site plan; OVERLEAF, FROM ABOVE: Exploded axonometric of plaza, canopy and escalators; exploded axonometric of platforms, ceiling systems and mezzanine; OVERLEAF RIGHT, ABOVE: Entry plaza from Vermont Avenue showing stainless steel canopy, an enclosed glass elevator to the left and glass pavers which channel light to the lower station levels; BELOW: Aerial view of entry plaza

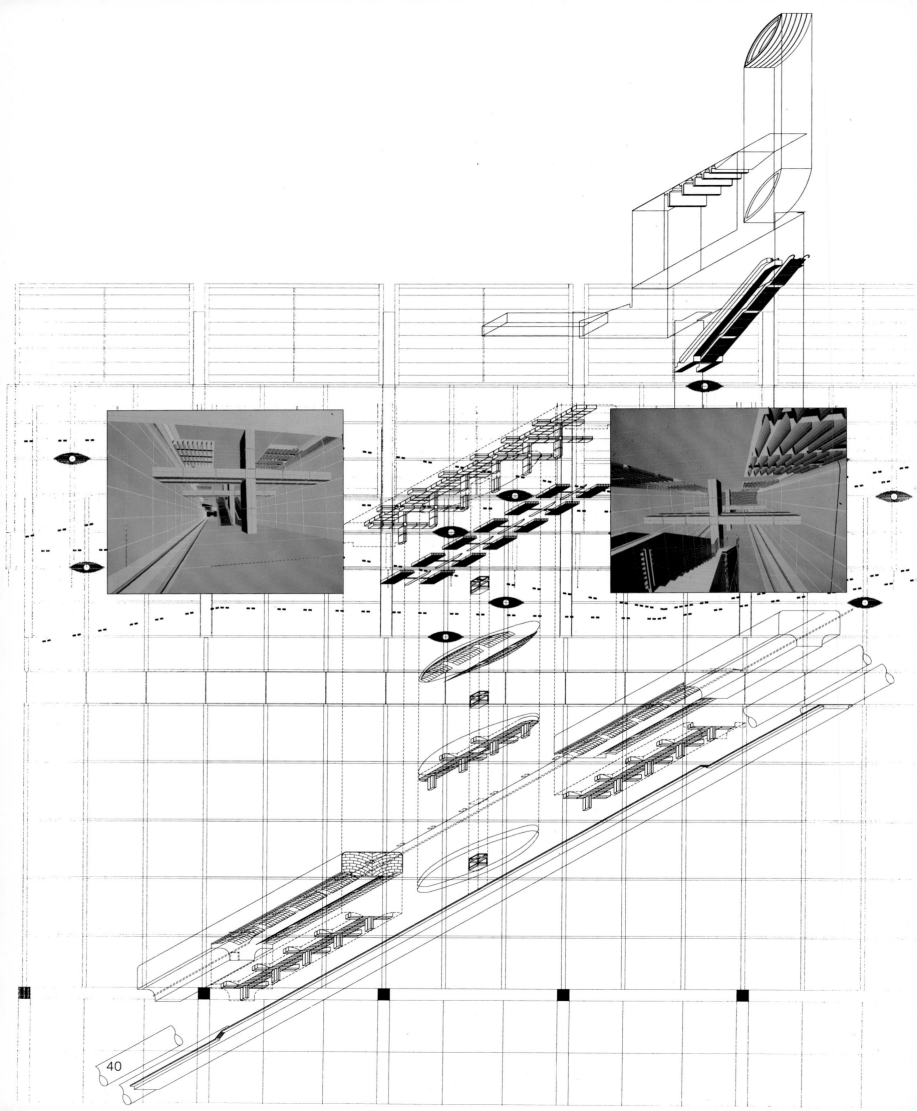

40

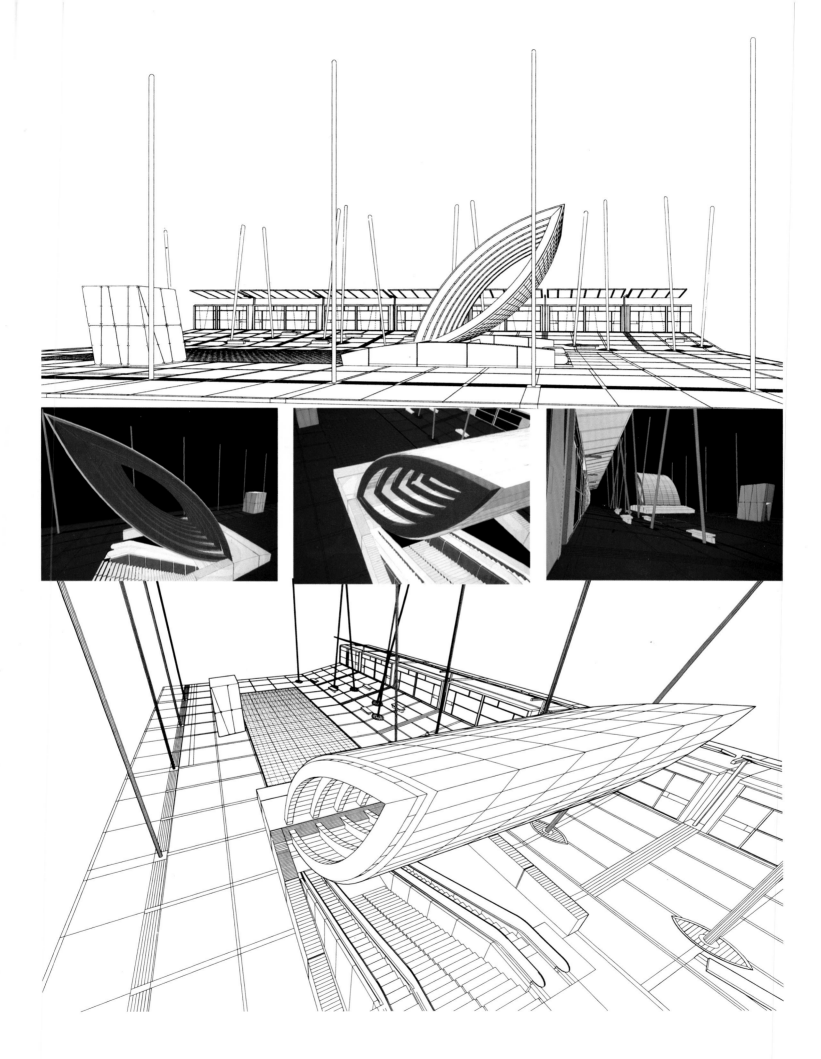

...Technical Block at
Bordeaux Airport seek to unify
...omplex through simplicity and clarity,
... conveying a high-performance
... befitting the aeronautical world.
... Control Tower directs the control
... towards the runways. Its supports
...ist of three elements which corre-
...d to the vertical connections feeding
... shaft of cables, the stairs and the
...ators. This supporting tripod consists
... oval leg in concrete positioned
...nd the control booth and two metal
...-dimensional supports, inclining ten
...es to ensure stability towards the
...These inclining structures are the
...and supports for the two elevators.
... technical rooms under the control
...n are conceived as a rigid box, self-
...orted by a periphery beam and re-
...ced by the floor. The roof of the
...ol booth consists of latticework,
...orted by very fine reinforcements in
...nes of certain joints in the glazing.
...empered and armoured glass is held
... the top and bottom by a mechanical
...em. It is separated from the roof by
...le joints to avoid the transmission of
...vibration. The vertical core is in
...rete with white lacquered aluminium
...ls. The metallic stairs behind are
...cted by a glass cage.
... Technical Block is modular to
...de total flexibility, and the entry hall
...anding on each floor connect all
... of each wing. Between the wings
...ourtyards which open onto the
...ays, framed by two grand windows
...ach floor. This offers a system of
...al references for the Technical Block
...mpassing the runways, aeroplanes
...control tower.
... city elevation is aligned with the
...ng airport facilities while the runway
...de takes the form of a tapering arc
...ding beyond the neighbouring
...rt facilities. This hull of white lac-
...ed aluminium presents a horizontal
...ation of solid and void, with terraces
...ing ... the runway at ... level.

*Site plan; OVERLEAF BELOW: Perspective view from the runway; OVERLEAF RIG...
FROM ABOVE: section through control room and control tower; section through c...
centre b...ildi... a...d elevation of con... wer.*

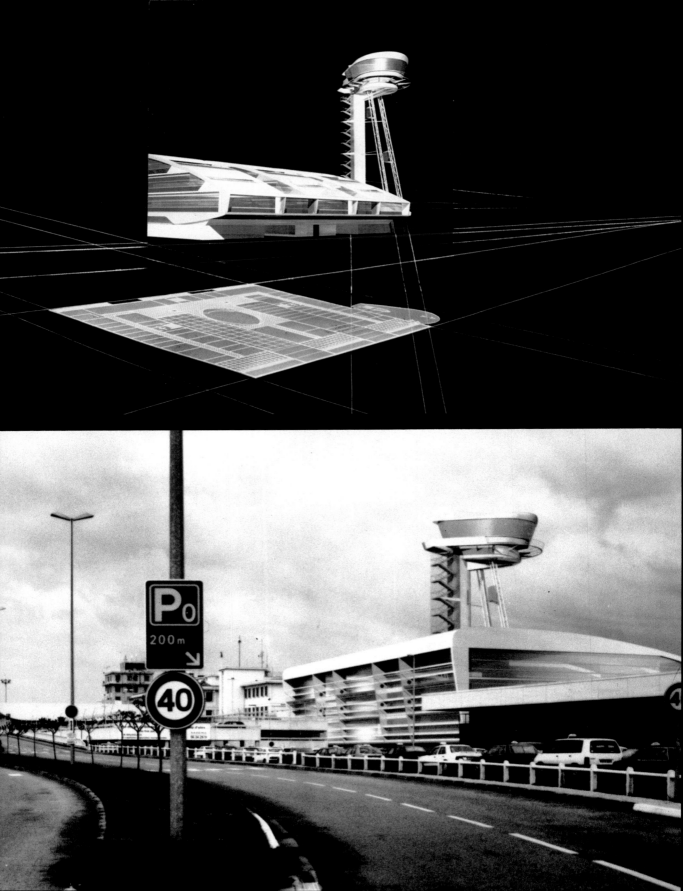

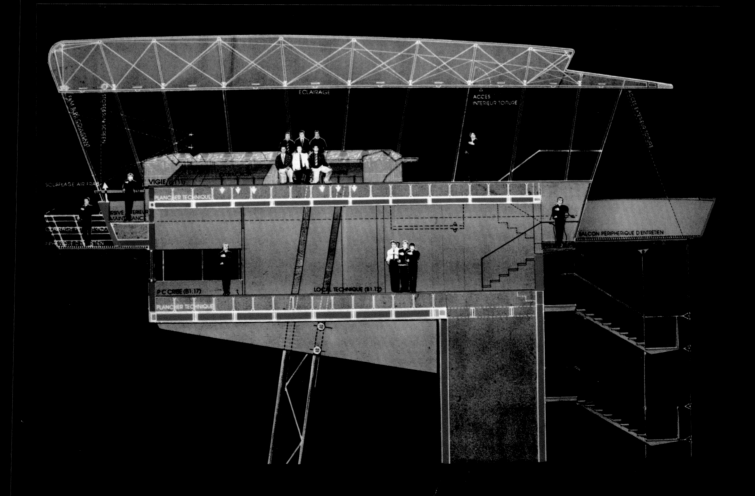

45

CENTRE D'EXPLOITATION DES AUTOROUTES
Nanterre

The Centre d'Exploitation des Autoroutes is part of a twofold plan on Highway A14 to connect an underground interchange and bridge with a viaduct.

In designing the viaduct the most important objective was to make it appear as light as possible, to create the best context for the park that was to be sited beneath. Thus the supports are brought closer at an optimal span; the edge of the roadway, the most visible element, is as fine as possible; and the split between the two carriageways is maintained, permitting light to reach the park below.

By its detachment from the ground, the Centre immediately affirms its integration with this highway system, in which it plays a pivotal role.

Conceived as floating, the Centre can be seen as a submarine, plunged into the flux of vehicles that constantly rushes by. Immersed under two carriageways of traffic, travelling to Paris and to the west, the entry hall and lookout post emerge. Here the volume of the hall slips between the two roadbeds of the highway to rise above the traffic and point its antenna towards the sky. This serves both as a signal of the gateway to the capital, and at the same time as the nerve centre of the highway.

The whole building is suspended from the supporting arcs of the viaduct, and to free the building from the sway and vibrations of the traffic the structure is as independent as possible. Two longitudinal caissons, one for each hall of the building, are carried between the two arcs which serve as supports for the viaduct and building. The caissons rest on supporting neoprene elements to create a barrier against the transmission of vibrations.

OPPOSITE, FROM ABOVE: West elevation of centre and section through highway; section; ABOVE: Detail section of centre and highway; BELOW: Detail section showing signage, structure and sound deflectors; OVERLEAF: Perspective

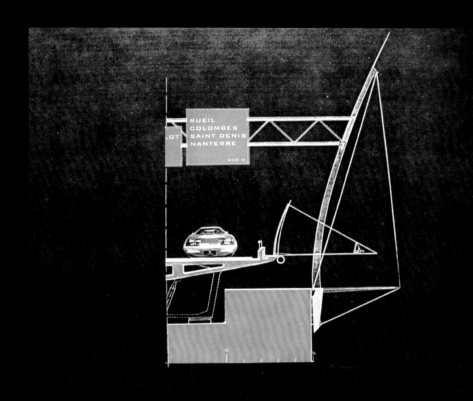

FENTRESS BRADBURN / BHJW

THE NEW SEOUL METROPOLITAN AIRPORT MAIN PASSENGER TERMINAL
Seoul

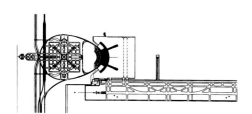

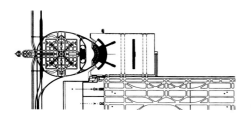

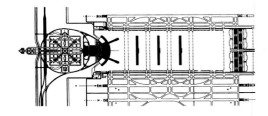

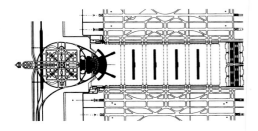

Expressive of the excitement of travel, the technology of our time, and the spirit of the people of Korea, the new Seoul Metropolitan Airport is a 21st-century gateway to Asia. The design presents a symbol that is clearly Korean in inspiration and execution, inspired by concepts and ideas such as traditional Korean architecture and the feeling of flight and motion.

The main terminal is radial in shape with two connected unit terminals which will provide a total of 46 gates. Seldom will the entire concept be seen in its totality, but rather experienced in a sequential fashion as one moves through the building. The design is composed of many parts that are assembled to form a whole, more like a city than a building. From the International Business Centre to the transportation terminal, passenger terminal and remote concourses, there are many variations in the architecture that come together to form spaces and articulate activities while achieving unity.

The main terminal building is organised around a 'great hall', a light filled, open space which will accommodate the landside People Mover System and Intra-Airport Transit stations. This provides a central location for transportation systems, customer service amenities and airport operations. All passengers and visitors will pass through this area affording a pleasant, convenient and humanistic experience. The form of the building and shape of the plan reinforces the orientation of the passenger, making the building easily understandable.

The roof forms of the main terminal are designed to express the spirit of flight and to respect the history of Korea. The repetitive arches of the ticket hall recall the structure of early biplanes, and the aerodynamically curved roof section reinforces the feeling of technology and the future. The up-sweeping curve of the concourse roof is also reminiscent of the graceful rooflines of traditional Korean palaces.

The design concept has been created with the philosophy that our future must be a proper marriage of technology and our environment. Thus natural daylight and interior landscaping have also been incorporated to provide a relaxed and pleasant travel experience for all passengers. In the selection of materials and finishes the architects have utilised pattern, texture and colour to symbolise the transition between earth and sky.

At the ticket hall in the main terminal, a space has been created where the outdoors has been brought inside. Skylights allow large amounts of daylight to flood into the space and interior landscaping and works of art accentuate the experience, while the exposed curved roof structure creates a feeling of lightness.

In the Arrivals level of the main terminal, skylights and open floors allow sunlight to reach even the lowest levels. All of the Concourses have large glass walls and skylights throughout creating an effect much like the Great Hall. This concept of incorporating large amounts of daylighting and open space makes the passengers' visit to New Seoul Metropolitan Airport a pleasant and memorable experience. Throughout the entire building, passengers are reminded of the wonder and excitement of flight.

Located on Yong Jong Do Island in the Yellow Sea, 30 miles west of Seoul City centre, the new airport is due for completion in the year 2000.

FROM ABOVE: Site plans showing phases I, II, III and IV (the ultimate build-out); OVERLEAF, FROM ABOVE: Approach to the main terminal; exterior of terminal showing loading bays; the 'great hall'; OVERLEAF RIGHT, FROM ABOVE RIGHT: Masterplan; typical phase I section; phase I section at 'great hall'; section at domestic concourse; section at east and west ends of main concourse

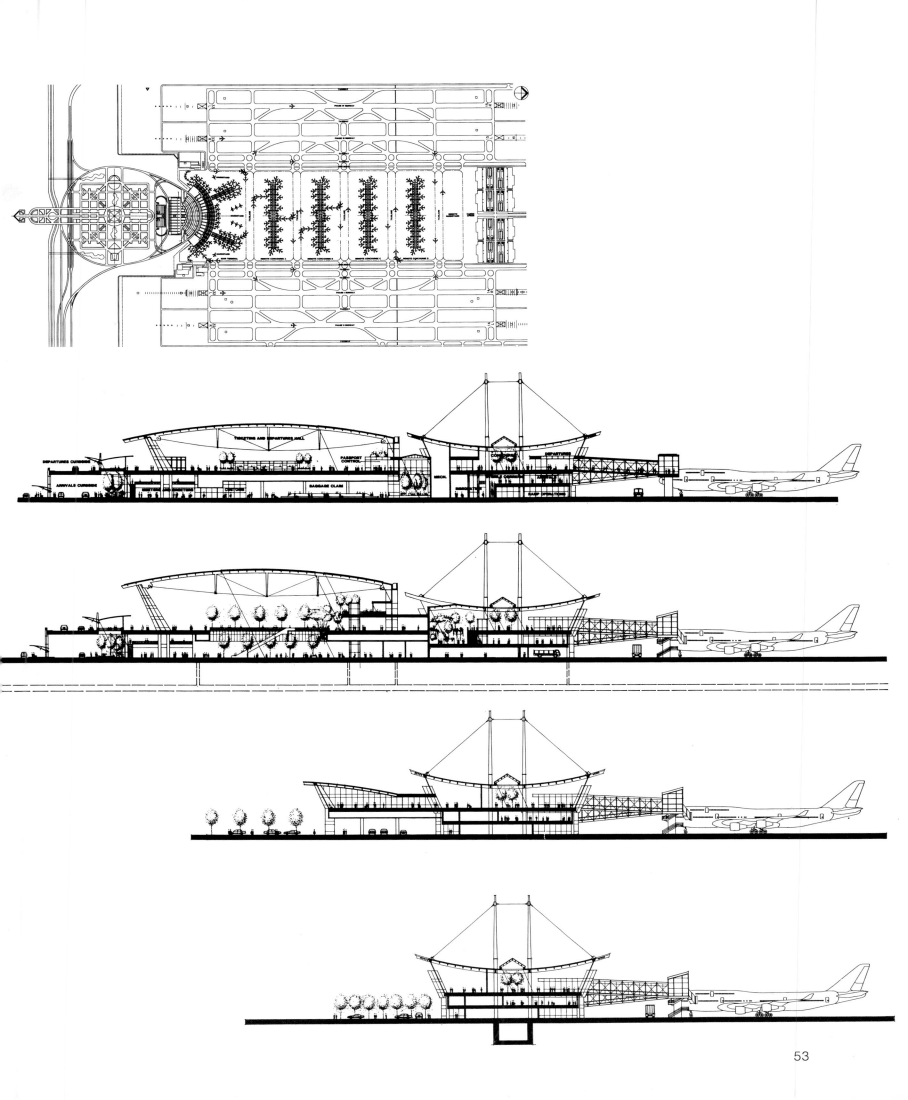

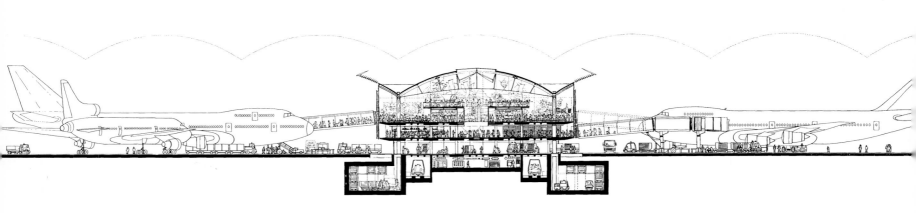

SIR NORMAN FOSTER AND PARTNERS
NEW AIRPORT AT CHEK LAP KOK
Hong Kong

The Hong Kong Government decided to invest in a new airport on Chek Lap Kok island to provide the cornerstone of ten major infrastructure projects.

Over 30 international groups, each consisting of architectural practices and engineers, responded to an initial call for interest. From these 38 were selected to tender and three were subsequently short-listed.

The objectives of the airport's design are to provide a modern airport terminal and concourse buildings for the 21st century to cater for the expected 35 million passengers per annum in 1997, and the potential 87 million passengers per annum in 2040.

The buildings will incorporate the best modern standards of safety, functional performance and quality and provide flexibility for future use. As the new buildings will provide passengers with their first impressions of Hong Kong, the design will strive to provide them with a pleasant and uplifting experience in an environment which is both convenient and comfortable.

All commercial and core facilities will be built in the centre of the terminal to allow ease of maintenance. There will be 39 air-bridge served gates. The airport will be able to accommodate new types of aircraft without affecting the day-to-day running of the complex.

Prefabricated steel will be used to construct the frame made up of 110 foot square modules on a repetitive and therefore flexible and economical grid. When finished, the first two terminal buildings and aircraft gate spine will be almost a mile long.

Sir Norman Foster and Partners' winning scheme will be ready for business in just four years, to replace the existing Kai Tak Airport by 1997 before the Chinese take over Hong Kong. The Chek Lap Kok airport is ten times bigger than Foster's Stansted which opened in 1991. The new airport island will cover 3,085 acres and be six kilometres long, there will be 30,000 square metres of space in the terminal and the airport will have an initial annual capacity for 1.32 million tonnes of cargo.

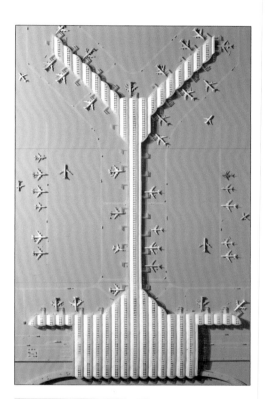

OPPOSITE BELOW: Cross section through satellite spine; BELOW: Longitudinal section

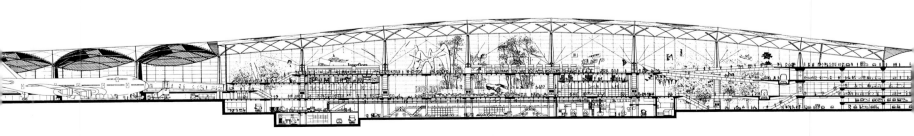

BILBAO METROPOLITAN RAILWAY
Spain

Sir Norman Foster and Partners provided the winning scheme in a limited competition, held by the Basque Government's Department of Transportation and Public Works, for the design of the Bilbao Metropolitan Railway in 1988.

The tunnel constitutes the main element in the project. Entry into the station cavern from surface level will be as simple and direct as possible by means of escalators. The 16-metre-wide station caverns will be constructed with a pre-cast concrete, permanent shuttering secondary structural liner as the predominant finished surface. The prefabricated components of the system (mezzanines, stairs, ticket barriers and lifts) are seen as separate elements within the main cavern and will be factory fabricated from durable materials such as stainless steel and glass. The smooth and refined quality of the prefabricated components offers a striking contrast to the weight and solidity of the cavern wall.

The main cavern is the heart of the system and all activities such as the purchase of tickets, information and access to the platform level occur within the cavern at mezzanine level. As the drama and enjoyment of the main cavern space is best appreciated when experiencing its full height and volume, the mezzanine areas (which hang from the cavern roof) are confined to a workable minimum.

All services are confined to 'plugs' at the ends of the cavern. A glazed end wall allows the control booth to have a full view of the station and is easily accessible to passengers. Ventilation ducts and electrical cables run below the platform and the trains are powered by an overhead catenary system.

Above ground, beautifully detailed glass enclosures announce the presence of the Metro below and invite people to use the system. Natural light filters into the access tunnel where artificial light highlights the escalators and stairs. At night the enclosures will glow from within.

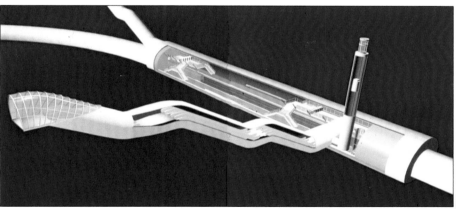

BELOW: CAD generation showing main cavern space

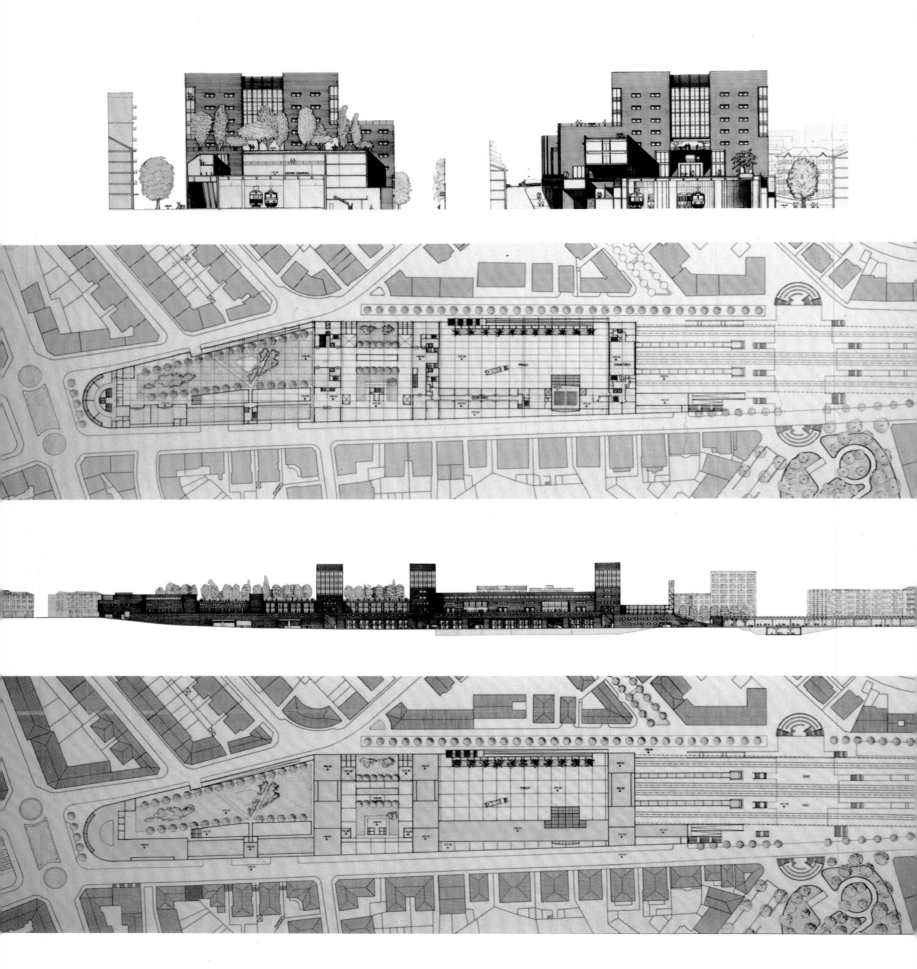

GREGOTTI ASSOCIATES
AMADORA CENTRAL STATION
Portugal

The city of Amadora which has developed around its railway station with a typical garden-city type fabric, lacks a defined urban centre precisely because of the barrier created by the railroad line itself which divides the settlement into two parts. The design proposes the construction of a longitudinal platform above the rail line for which access is provided by a system of ramps and escalators. Upon the platform a series of public spaces with both plantings and pavement is to be alternated with three tall blocks for important public functions. Particular attention has been dedicated to the design and volumetric arrangement of the edifices in an attempt to provide an urban character for the facades and to make the strategic points of crossing evident.

The project proposes the restructuring of the central station in Amadora, covering a large railroad area, augmenting the commercial and service industries facilities of the city. The central idea of the project is to create three large urban spaces which are highly integrated within the city itself.

The square is directly connected to the station by means of two escalators. Special attention was paid to the design of the systems of access to the square with ramps for the handicapped, escalators and lifts. The shopping centre has been conceived as an arcade of shops arranged along two orthogonal paths. The multi-level parking facilities, easily accessed from the bordering streets, also include the delivery and disposal areas and department store areas for the indoor shopping centre, with a hanging garden which becomes an integral part of the entire urban system. The project is to be constructed in three phases.

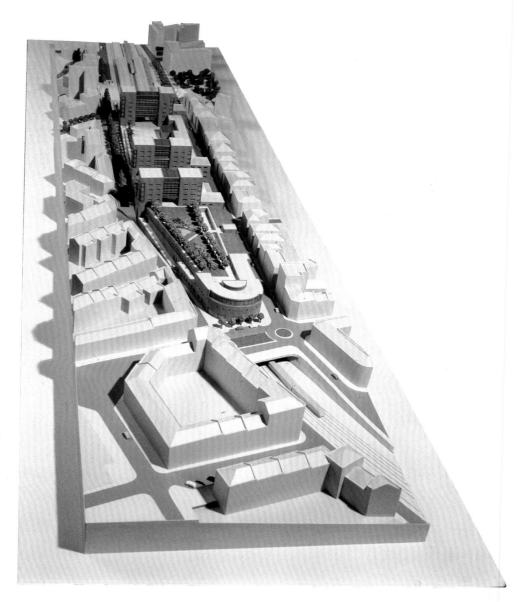

OPPOSITE, FROM ABOVE: Sections; typical floor plan; elevation; roof plan

NICHOLAS GRIMSHAW & PARTNERS

PIER 4A
Heathrow, London

The demand for a new satellite and piers for domestic passengers at London's Heathrow Airport presented gruelling demands of both site and brief for the architects, but they were also concerned to demonstrate that airport corridors need not be characterless and cluttered, and to show that the quality of the architecture need not decline on the journey from terminal to aeroplane.

The new piers are attached to Terminal One and serve domestic flights, flights to Belfast and flights within the Common Travel Area (CTA) which includes the Republic of Ireland and the Channel Islands. Before they were built, inadequate facilities meant that passengers had to endure lengthy journeys on foot or by bus from terminal to plane. The development includes a new terminal and pier providing a direct link to both existing and new air bridges for access to the planes, refurbishment of the existing pier to provide a new lounge for Belfast passengers, and a 'nose' building which incorporates baggage reclaim and links to and from the new facilities and Terminal 1.

The brief included a number of major design constraints. Passengers to each of the three types of destination have different security and customs arrangements; this means that, although they share the piers, their circulation has to be rigorously segregated. The new pier had to be built over an existing airside road whilst other elements of the development had to be tied into the existing complex web of airport circulation and operations. Further complications arose from the requirement to maintain visual and radar sight lines and headroom clearances above the airside road, as well as the demands of airport safety, security and airport and airline operations and costs. The route for CTA passengers passes through two elevated corridors linked by a circular duty-free and waiting area, which is built on the previously unused centre of a traffic roundabout. As well as segregating passengers more gracefully,

this layout simplified the phased construction, so that the CTA pier could open while other phases were still being constructed. Both the CTA and domestic flights are connected to a building which, shaped like an aeroplane nose, houses the baggage reclaim and customs for CTA passengers, and leads domestic passengers to and from the main Terminal One building.

The main pier building has been split across its short dimension into two sections, with five of the nine gates dedicated to CTA passengers and four to domestic flights. Each section can be reached without passing through the other. Its structure is a creative response to its constraints. Given that it is confined by minimum and maximum height restrictions, and by a fixed width, a structure that used depth effectively was essential. The solution was to employ steel portal frames spanning the road beneath the pier, with steel beams running between the frames supporting a concrete floor. This creates a platform which in turn carries a very light steel frame. The design has been devised to constantly help orientate the passengers as they move through the terminal.

Departing passengers will see the noses of their trains from the station concourse, and then pass through a linear progression of ticket, security and passport checks to the waiting area, from where they will rise by one of two escalators or a travelator to the point nearest their seat place. For arriving passengers, the direction of the travelator and one of the escalators is reversed, taking passengers down to a ground-floor arrivals' concourse, which opens directly on to the road outside.

RIGHT: Site plan; PAGE 63, BELOW LEFT: Down-view axonometric of elevated pier; PAGE 63, BELOW RIGHT: Cross section through elevated pier showing the lighting and services boom, curved window, rooflight and seating; Suspended lighting boom incorporating uplighting and downlighting, public address speakers, emergency address speakers, emergency lighting and wireways

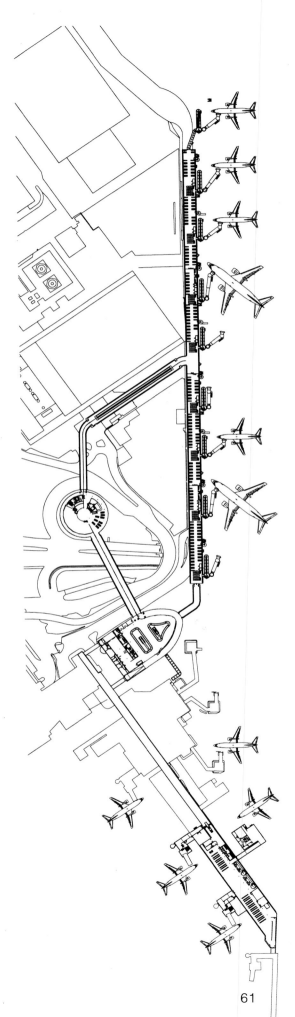

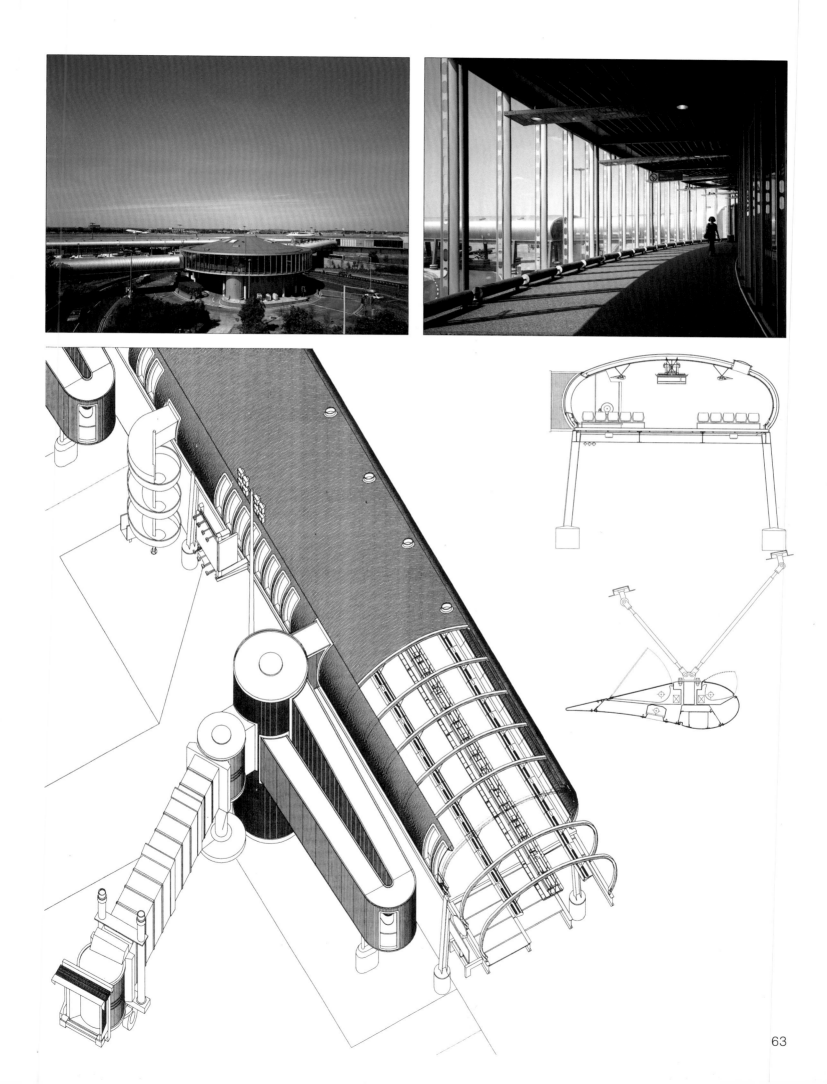

WATERLOO INTERNATIONAL TERMINAL
Lambeth

The Terminal will offer facilities similar to those of an airport, but in the centre of the capital. Seen as a gateway to Europe it was important that the Terminal should have its own identity and the design concept has particularly stressed the distinction between the Terminal and domestic services at Waterloo. It has the capacity to handle up to fifteen million passengers a year with the appropriate amenities of car parking, a departure lounge, ticket hall areas, customs, immigration and all of the necessary back-up facilities.

The objective was to create a stream-lined terminal that would allow passengers to pass through with the minimum fuss at maximum speed. Ramps and mechanical conveyors allow passengers to move with ease through the different levels of the building as well as ensuring full access for the disabled. It was imperative to British Rail that the terminal should provide a high quality environment even during times of heavy demand.

The building form is determined by the turning radius of the new trains and the confines of the site. The five new tracks dictated both the complex geometry and shape of the whole building. The terminal can be broken down into five constituent parts. The first is the basement car park constructed from a heavily reinforced concrete box which forms a raft spanning the shallow Underground lines immediately below, forming the foundation for the Terminal. A two-storey viaduct sits on this concrete box which supports the platforms and within it are two floors of passenger accommodation including the arrivals and departures facilities. The third element is the work undertaken on the existing station. Many of the brick vaults below which were badly managed during the Second World War have been refurbished. They will house all the essential back up operations, including an extensive catering suite. The roof forms the fourth section of the project and has been one of the greatest challenges in design terms. It extends the full length of the four-hundred-metre trains,

providing shelter for the eight hundred passengers who will use each train. Half of its length sits on the new viaduct that contains the passenger facilities and half on the widened viaduct that carries the new trains into Waterloo.

It was considered essential that the function of the building should be integral to the design, serving to demystify the building, making it easier for passengers to use, and conveying the exhilaration of travel, particularly in the newly designed train. Because of the track configuration, the most western train facing London and the Thames is on the edge of the viaduct and so the amount of glazing on this side of the building is maximised. It was important to resolve how to enclose a variable shape with spans reducing from fifty to thirty-five metres which also follows a sinuous and variable curve.

Because of the asymmetrical geometry of platforms, the centre pin is moved to one side allowing the arch to rise steeply on the west to clear the structural envelope of the train and a more gentle incline over the platforms on the east. The skin on this skeleton demanded fresh thinking. Because of the twisting nature of the structure, a standard glazing system would have been extremely expensive. In addition, thousands of different sized and shaped components would have made construction within the tight time frame extremely difficult. Instead, a different 'loose fit' approach was adopted, where a limited number of different sized glass sheets are used. The selection of materials has been given careful thought, both for longevity and ease of maintenance. British Rail has asked for a building which, with regular maintenance, should have a design life of over a hundred years.

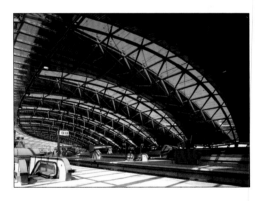

OVERLEAF ABOVE, FROM L TO R: Cross sections; roof bay plans on two different grid lines showing how different each segment is; OVERLEAF CENTRE: Exploded axonometric; OVERLEAF BELOW: Section

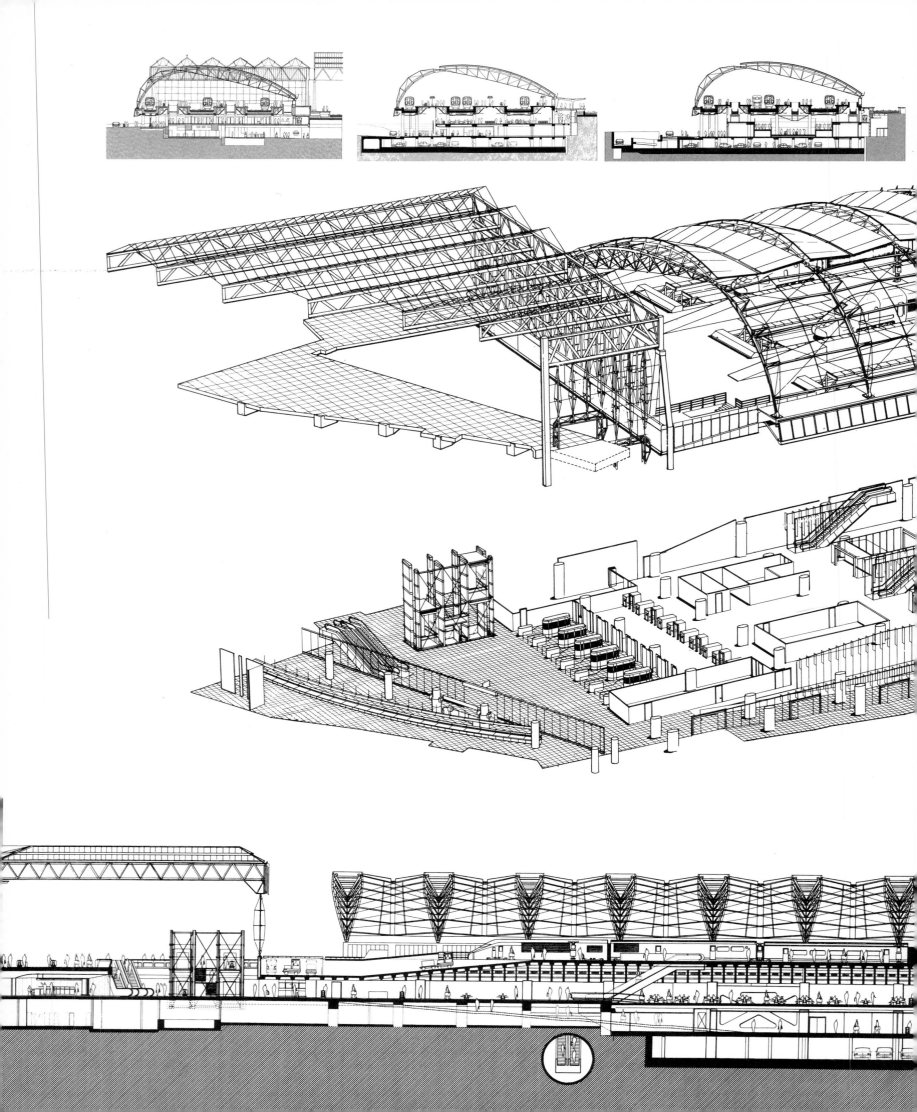

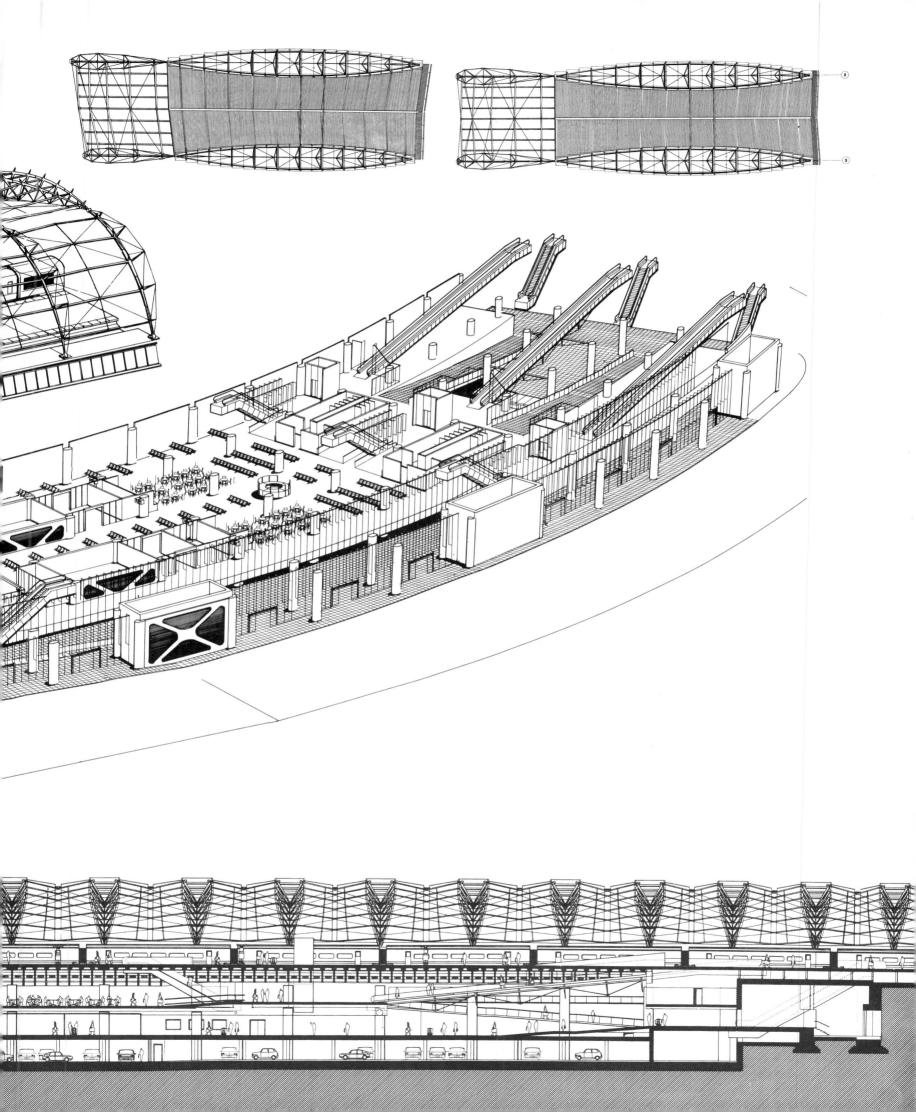

INGENHOVEN OVERDIEK PETZINKA

CIRCULAR TERMINAL FOR THE COLOGNE / BONN AIRPORT
Germany

The development of an airport of such dimensions always requires a basic analysis of the need and functions of people in airports, as well as of buildings and infrastructures accorded to human scales. IOP's aim was to plan an analogous airport characterised by the possibility to experience and see all the structures.

The existing structure is harmoniously integrated into the concept of the concentric circle. The original building formerly gestured outward. This has now been turned inward by the extension buildings, with the former interior area becoming the centre.

The airport concept embraces three worlds of experience: the centre, which is conceived of as a biotope, the transparent terminal rings and the external ring of the passenger gates and their waiting aircraft. In the apron, the terminal looks like a glazed, hovering ring, to which the passenger gates are attached radially. The separation between the land and air sides is created by a transparent wall with its functionally necessary apertures, arranged radially. The public lounge adjacent to the land side links the three terminals and encompasses the concentric ring with a glass skin.

A green area opens up to the passenger offering an attractive and unique impression also serving as an ecological, economic and energy resource. The cable-web construction of the lounge area is extrapolated as a transparent roofing over the drop-off ring at the departure level. On this level the passengers are directly guided from the drop-off point in the inner circle of the complex to the boarding area in the outer circle. After entering into the lounge with daylight and plants, they are faced with the check-in and ticket counters; in the background they can see the waiting space and the aircraft adjacent to the passenger gates.

Beside the terminal the runway is directly experienced by the passenger and it is accentuated and framed against the functional grid of taxiways and roads.

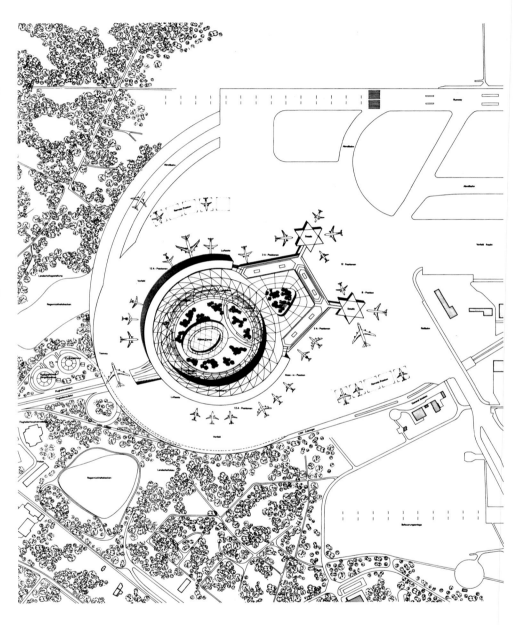

Site plan

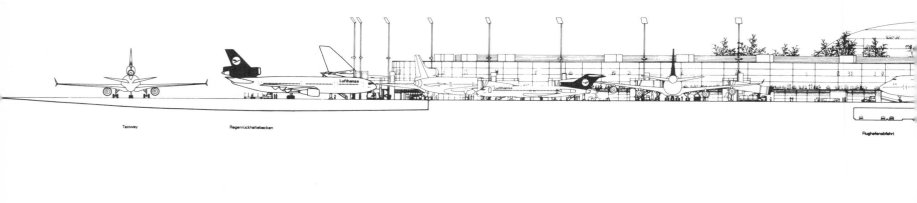

Taxiway   Regenrückhaltebecken   Flughafenabfahrt

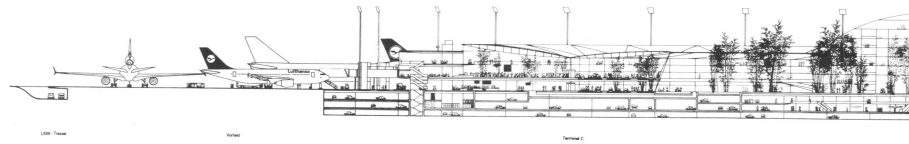

LKW - Trasse   Vorfeld   Terminal C

70

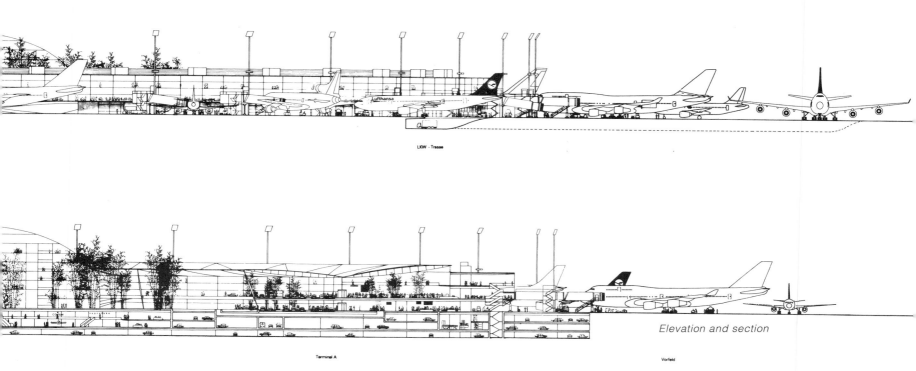

Elevation and section

71

PAUL LUKEZ
THE ROLLING BRIDGE INITIATIVE
Boston

The Rolling Bridge Initiative (RBI) is a non-profit organisation that seeks to save and reuse the 'Rolling Bridge', a forgotten railway drawbridge spanning Boston's Fort Point Channel Basin, currently slated for removal as part of the project to depress the Central Artery. PLA&D collaborated with Mike Tyrrell of RBI to reactivate the underused industrial landscape surrounding the Rolling Bridge by transforming the bridge into a type of time piece, a trace of past urban connections and potential future links.

When it was in use, the three parallel sections of the drawbridge pivoted open with the help of counterweights. Relocated, in an upright position, adjacent to their original site, and set back from the channel's edge, the bridge sections can be viewed at grade or from an elevated walkway perched 14 feet above the channel. This walkway is part of a proposed network of paths and parks that will link the residential South End with the Fort Point Channel warehouse district. A pair of offset scrims, curtains approximately 40 feet high and 300 feet long, is hung alongside the elevated walkway. The scrims receive the changing patterns of light and shadow cast by the bridge

and are themselves reflected in the channel's surface. The three-dimensional bridge transforms into the two-dimensional shapes that appear on the scrims. Viewers then re-experience the bridge's three-dimensional form as they travel across the elevated walkway, under and alongside the shapes appearing on the curtain. Perception of the bridge, as the shapes are modified by the movement of sun and clouds, would shift throughout the day and the season.

The site recaptures a lost physical and historical connection to the urban landscape: the bridge segments face downtown Boston and align with the granite footings of an earlier bridge that previously existed on the site. Pedestrians walking through and between the bridge segments on a series of stairways experience the superstructure as no one could during the operation of the bridge, thus becoming familiar with the patterns and materials of an urban infrastructure. The bridge also serves as a prominent marker for commuters travelling on the highways overlooking the site. From all points of view, the Rolling Bridge will be transformed from a discarded piece of Boston's infrastructure into a gateway and icon of the industrial era.

Conceptual sketch

RENZO PIANO
KANSAI INTERNATIONAL AIRPORT PASSENGER TERMINAL BUILDING
Japan

When the competition for the terminal building at the new Kansai International Airport was launched in 1988, the artificial island in Osaka Bay on which it was to be sited was still under construction. Renzo Piano Building Workshop's winning scheme, with the aerodynamic sweep of its gleaming metallic roof, however, provided an inspired embodiment of aircraft technology and the logical passenger movements and services which were required.

The Passenger Terminal Building is composed of the main terminal building and the wing, which is dedicated to departure/arrival lounges connected to 41 direct boarding bridges, with an automated guideway system running its length to carry passengers to their destination. The main terminal houses passenger facilities such as passport control and check-in, and has been planned so that passenger circulation is limited to horizontal (check-in procedures) and vertical (transfer) movement. Piano has placed great emphasis on achieving clarity of orientation for passengers, and to this end transparency is a major aim of the design. Passengers arriving at the airport by either road or ferry/hydrofoil enter the building at the 'canyon', a hall which runs the 275-metre length of the main terminal and allows passengers to move longitudinally and vertically in landscaped surroundings.

The distinctive form of the Passenger Terminal originates in the aerodynamic curve of the air flow designed to control the internal environment of the vast top floor, while the visibility required by the control tower defines the boundaries of its form: its peak and edges.

This project by the Renzo Piano Building Workshop, Japan KK, was in collaboration with Ove Arup & Partners International Ltd; Nikken Sekkei Ltd; Aeroports de Paris; Japan Airport Consultants Inc. Competition design by Renzo Piano Building Workshop, Paris (Renzo Piano, Noriaki Okabe) and Ove Arup & Partners International Ltd (Peter Rice, Tom Barker)

OPPOSITE LEFT, FROM ABOVE: Main roof truss; open air duct; exploded axonometric roof system; RIGHT: Masterplan

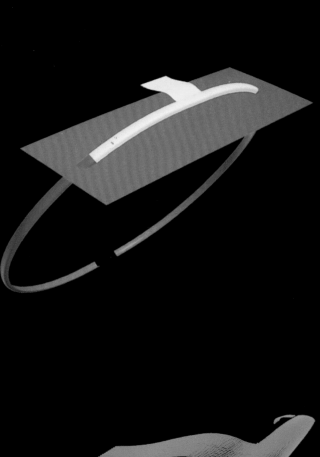
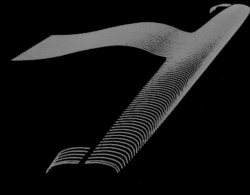
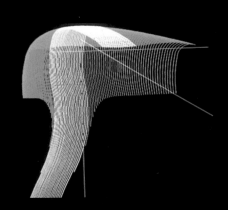

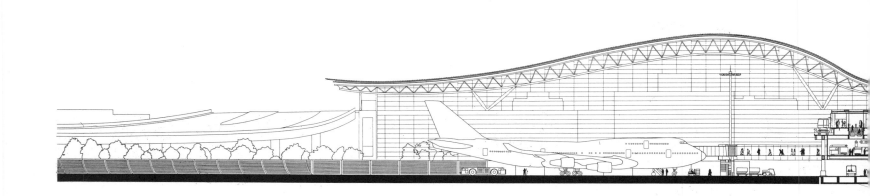

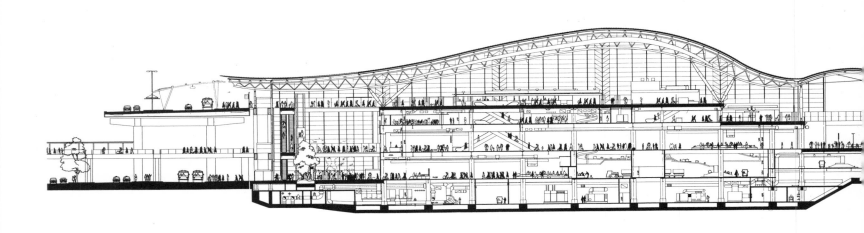

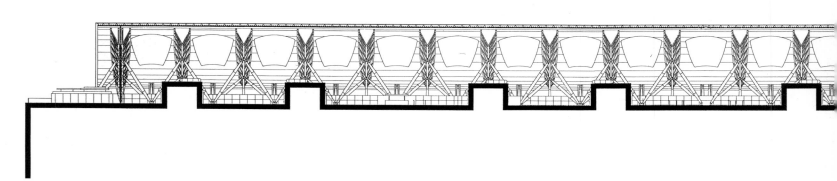

FROM ABOVE: Wing section; section through main terminal building; fourth floor section

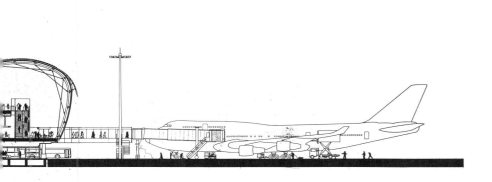

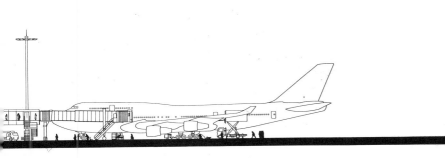

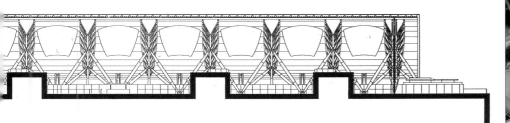

RICHARD ROGERS PARTNERSHIP
MARSEILLES INTERNATIONAL AIRPORT
France

Marseille-Provence is France's second largest airport after Paris, with an average of 4.5 million passengers per year, located equidistant between Marseilles and Aix-en-Provence on an inland lake which was the site of the first flight of a flying boat. By 1988, the projected rate of expansion in air traffic was such that a long term strategy was necessary with a development plan that would permit expansion of up to 15 million passengers a year.

The existing airport created a number of problems. Several separate developments clustered around the original building designed by Pouillon in the late 1950s, formed the terminal for international traffic. Another building which catered for national flights was linked by a high level walkway and the processing of passengers from car to plane had become confusing.

The architects' prime objectives were to create a strong new image by which the airport could be identified whilst fulfilling the constraints of the complex brief. It was required that all arriving and departing passengers should be separated once airside, and that security checks could be provided for in future. To cope with the unpredictable variations in air traffic the project had to be capable of phased development, with the minimum possible disruption to the smooth functioning of the airport.

The solution adopted by the architects was based upon a linear expansion airside, and a new central focus for landside activities. This linear solution was adopted because it conformed to the existing apron layout of taxiways and runways, and would permit a phased development with minimum inconvenience to both passengers and staff.

The masterplan devised by the architects can be divided into the following three distinct elements: the tube, national and international 'darses' and the *coeur*; The tube is a high level walkway which permits the physical separation of arriving and departing passengers. Built just in front of the existing departure lounges it provides an architectural continuity to the airside facade. The tube is linked to pre-passerelles – structures which serve as the interface between the high level tube for arriving passengers, the departure lounge at first floor level and the air bridges connecting with the aircraft. Each pre-passerelle can serve up to two aircraft simultaneously through the use of automatically controlled glazed sliding doors.

Getting up to the tube by means of an escalator, arriving passengers have an opportunity to orientate themselves directly after leaving the aircraft. As they walk along the length of the tube there are splendid views over the airport and surrounding hills through a fully glazed facade before descending to reclaim their baggage at ground level.

The darses are new buildings at each end of the airport providing additional capacity to the existing departure lounges and aircraft stands. The continuity of the airside facade is maintained, with the tube absorbed as a mezzanine into these buildings, and the pre-passerelles continuing to project forwards into the apron. The buildings are designed to be capable of linear expansion up to the final projected capacity of the airport.

At the centre of the development is the proposed heart of the airport which will form the focus for all landside activities. Currently a void between the national and international terminals, this will be covered by large lightweight parasol structures which appear to float over the surrounding buildings. This, together with the strong imagery, links the heterogeneous group of buildings. The parasols are constructed from two concentric circular tubes, the lower suspended by rods from the steel mast. Located at the intersection point for arriving and departing passengers, the heart forms the commercial centre to the airport. Shops are located within free-standing blocks that can be adapted as is necessitated.

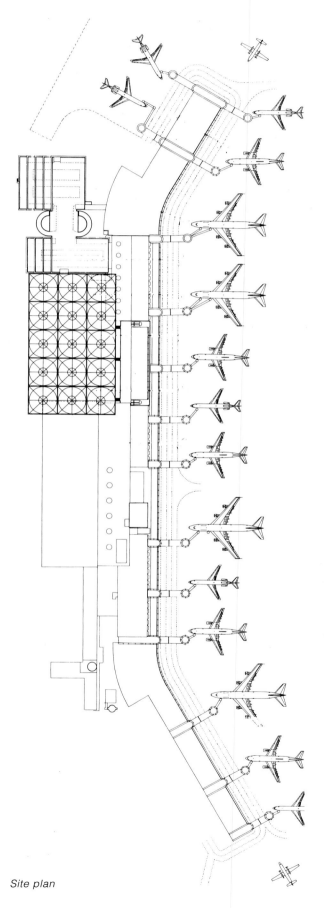

Site plan

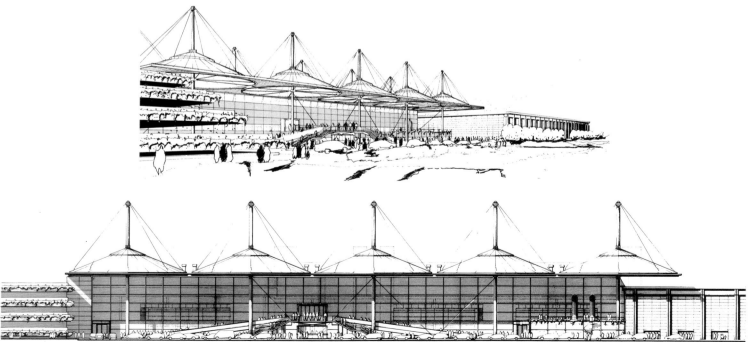

CENTRE L to R: Perspective of entrance; interior perspective; BELOW L to R: Entrance elevation; cross section

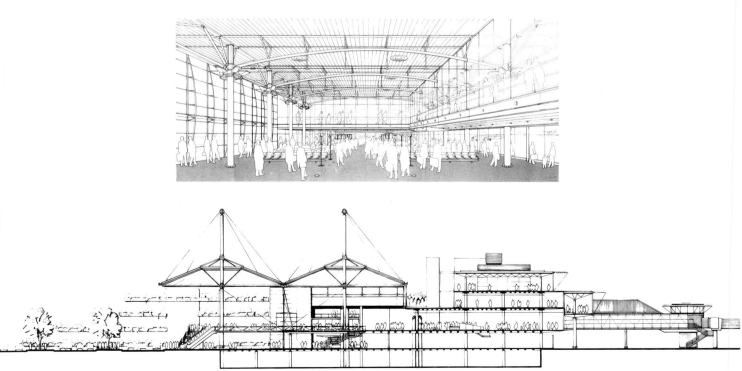

BERLIN U5 BAHNHOF LINE
Germany

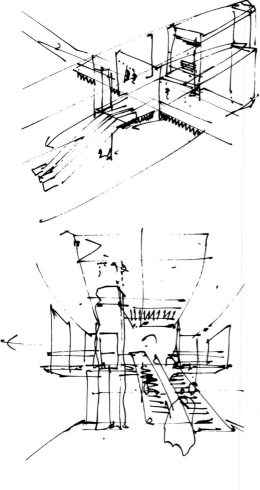

The Richard Rogers Partnership won a limited international competition to design a proto-typical station for the Berlin U5 Bahnhof line. The line currently serves East Berlin from Alexanderplatz and is expected to be upgraded and integrated within the greater Metropolitan underground network. The architects' proposals concentrate on integrating the stations, through a linking sequence of spaces from street to train, into the city's streetscape.

A variety of street level curved glass shelters are designed to house the differing functions of ticket offices, information displays, disabled access, lifts etc. These form the first interface with the passenger who is led along landscaped ramps and staircases into the station proper; revealing, surprisingly, naturally lit platforms with views to the street above. The result is an atmosphere of an extension of the street rather than of a disassociated underground world.

This transformation of the typical underground system was achieved by taking advantage of the proximity of the station roof to street level. The platforms are opened up to natural daylight with street level skylights taking the form of shallow ellipses. No longer entombed beneath the ground the platforms become sheltered street spaces by day and welcoming glowing rooms by night.

FROM ABOVE: Initial sketch; entrance sketch; longitudinal section

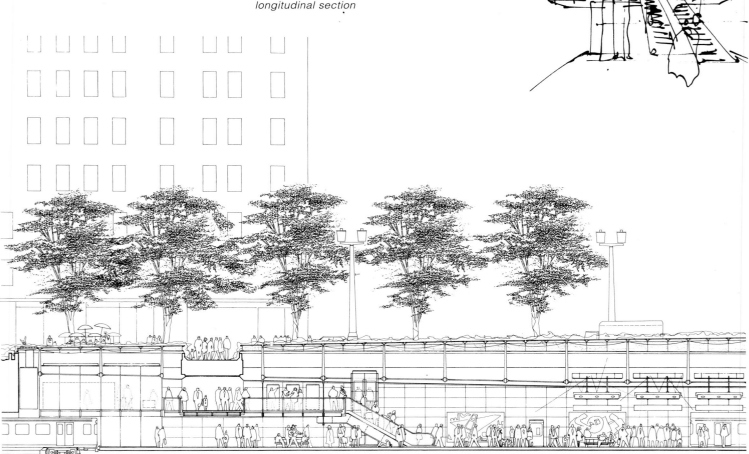

SHIN TAKAMATSU

·SHICHIRUIKO TERMINAL
Nima-cho, Shimane Prefecture

The news of a meteorite falling on to a residence in Mihonoseki, Shimane Prefecture on 10 December, 1992, spread rapidly over the whole nation.

Was it an early present from Santa Claus or a message from UFO? This eight kilogramme object obliged a small town along the Japanese sea to send a message to the universe.

Mihonoseki is a port city which sends 170,000 passengers to Okinoshima Island each year. Takamatsu & Associates' architectural intention was to build a gate for passengers and a machine to encourage more traffic. The terminal also contains public space for interaction between passengers and city residents.

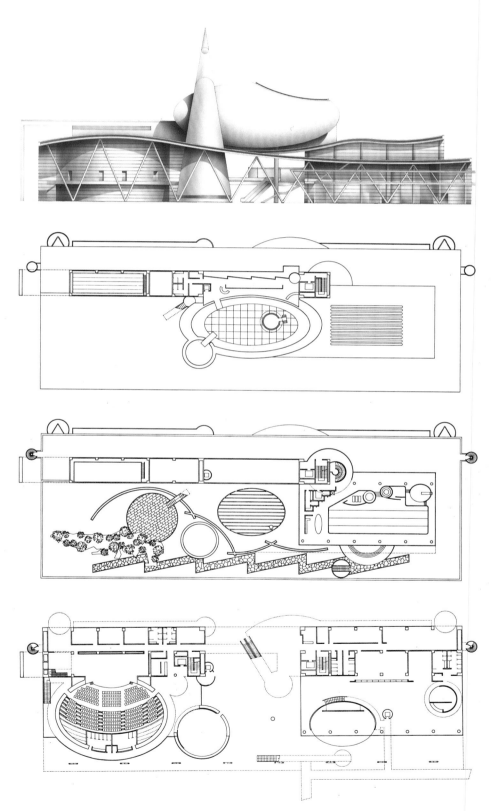

FROM ABOVE: Perspective; fourth floor plan; third floor plan; first floor plan

FUTURE PORT CITY

An air traffic prognosis was issued by Japan Airlines (JAL) in 1990, following years of preparatory analysis. As a result Shin Takamatsu & Associates was granted a contract to plan an airport that was to meet requirements in the year 2050.

The structure asked for in the JAL report was required to satisfy the demand for proper accommodation of new technologies, as extrapolated into the next millennium. The architects' response to JAL's programme was to concentrate attention on the probable changes on the perception of space and time, as would be generated by the revolution of speed.

ABOVE: Site plan; BELOW: Section

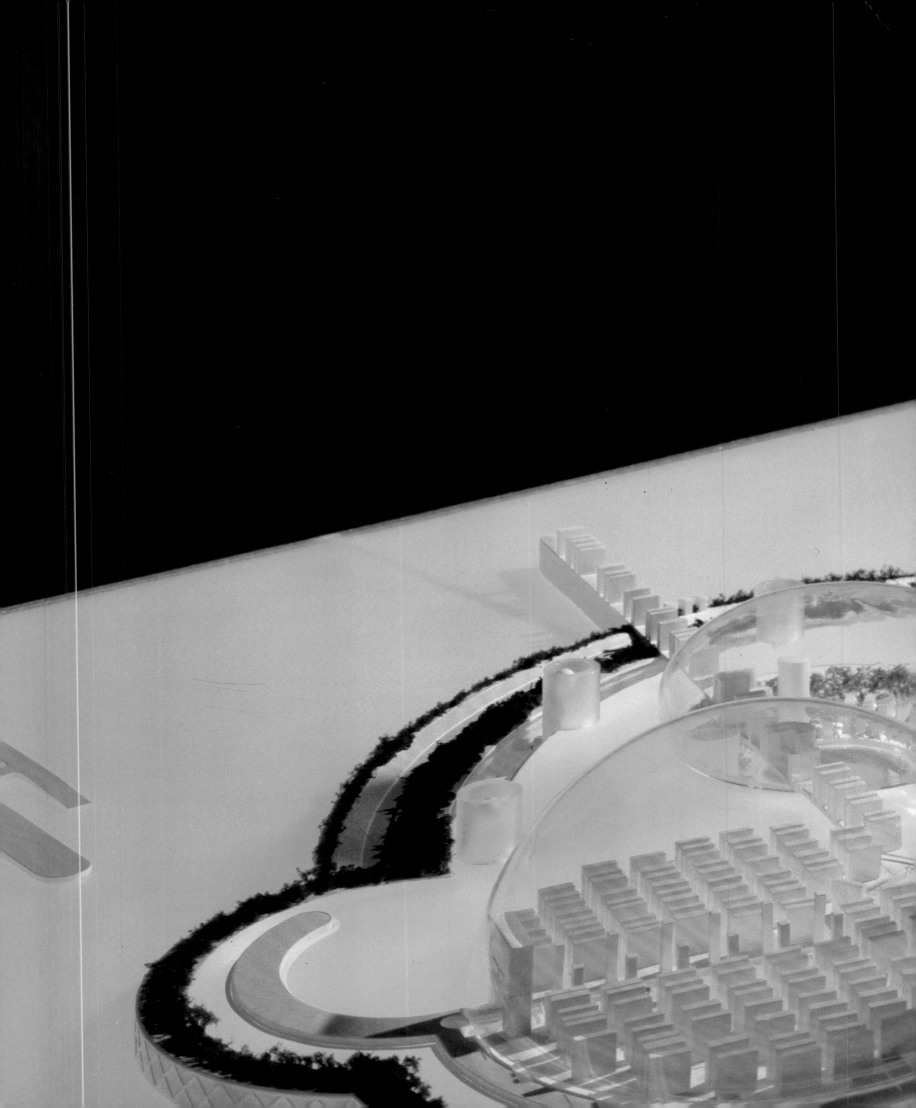

MICHAEL WILFORD AND PARTNERS
ABANDO PASSENGER INTERCHANGE
Bilbao, Spain

Although strategically located, the existing Abando Station and its associated plateau of rail tracks currently separates the medieval and nineteenth-century quarters of the city and contributes little to the amenity of adjacent neighbourhoods. The new Abando Passenger Interchange incorporates a series of positive urban interventions to counteract these deficiencies. They include: a public plaza; a series of new buildings set in public gardens; grand colonnades flanking Calle Amezaga and Calle Bailen; and a network of pedestrian routes between them to establish a vibrant new heart to the city.

The Interchange comprises three transportation facilities: a bus station for suburban and inter-urban bus services; a new and enlarged RENFE railway station; and a new FEVE railway station. These facilities are layered and linked directly to the Metro and adjacent streets to provide convenient passenger access and connections. The Interchange also contains a retail concourse, World Trade Centre, hotel and offices. Removal of the station plateau and relocation of the RENFE and FEVE Stations to the centre of the site allows construction of new buildings containing shops, offices and numerous entrances to the Interchange, thereby transforming them into active urban streets.

The trio of contrasting outdoor spaces for public assembly and relaxation – the plaza, station roof garden and triangular World Trade Centre Garden – contributes to the sequence of landscaped public recreation spaces along the river and across the city centre as proposed in the City Development Plan.

The new Abando Plaza is the forecourt of the Interchange, a new centre of social activity in Bilbao and a place for visitors to orientate themselves before exploring the city. It is enclosed by the existing RENFE Station entrance, stock exchange, Santander Station and north facade of the Interchange. Glazed arcades encircle the plaza and provide weather protected connections to the Metro escalators situated in a new ground level loggia in the RENFE Station entrance. Centrally positioned overlooking the plaza, the glass cube is the entrance pavilion of the Interchange and contains lifts and escalators to all levels. It is the point of arrival and departure, a place to wait for friends, visit the cinema or have lunch in one of the high level restaurants overlooking the gardens and city. Tilted, to invite entry, the pavilion will register the presence of the Interchange on the city skyline.

The World Trade Centre tower is the focus of the Interchange for bus and car passengers arriving through the San Francisco Gateway. The hotel and new post office building enclose the long sides of the triangular garden. Three new housing blocks, with private courtyard gardens and underground car parking, relate in form and scale to buildings in the adjacent San Francisco quarter.

The new Interchange will bring many benefits to the city of Bilbao. It will incorporate existing disparate bus and train passenger termini into one central facility connected to the Metro with consequent ease of access and connections between them. It will allow direct passenger and tourist access to business, social and shopping activities in central Bilbao. It will forge strong connections between the medieval and nineteenth-century city and revitalisation of the central area by the incorporation of a public plaza, hotel, World Trade Centre, offices, shopping arcades and public gardens. The Interchange will replace existing service and industrial facilities adjacent to the existing Abando Station with business, social and cultural amenities more appropriate to the city centre location. The relocation of the FEVE Station and the diversion of the rail service currently terminating at La Naja Station into the new RENFE Station will allow growth of the city to the edge of the river and introduce a promenade and other public facilities.

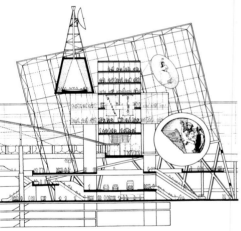

ABOVE: Cross section; OVERLEAF, FROM ABOVE L TO R: Axonometric at bus station and plaza level; axonometric at RENFE track level; axonometric at retail/FEVE level; axonometric at garden level; OVERLEAF CENTRE, L TO R: Plan of RENFE tracks; plan of retail and FEVE level; plan of park and garden; OVERLEAF BELOW: Site section

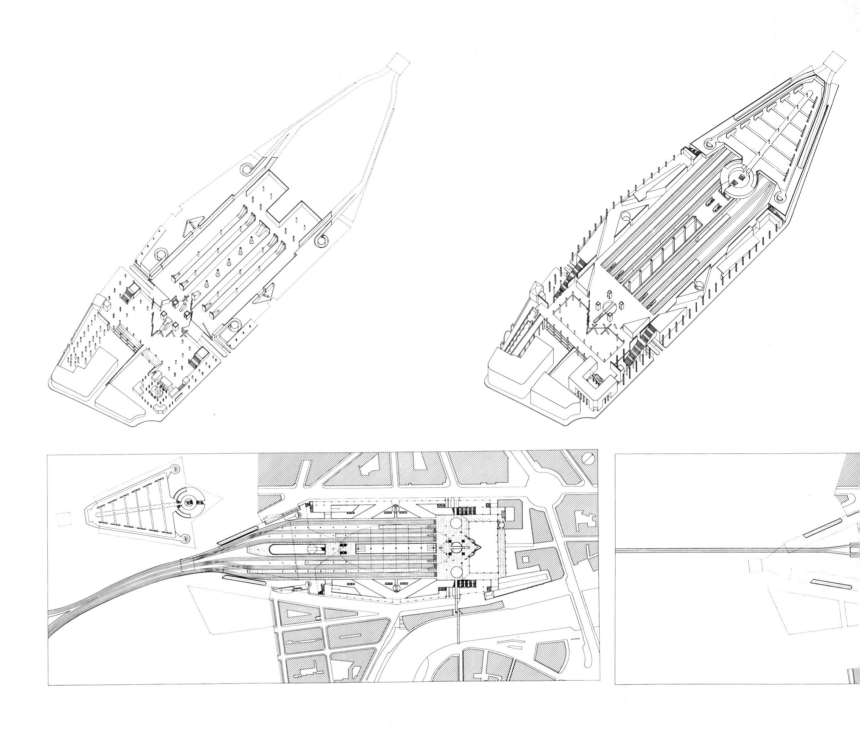

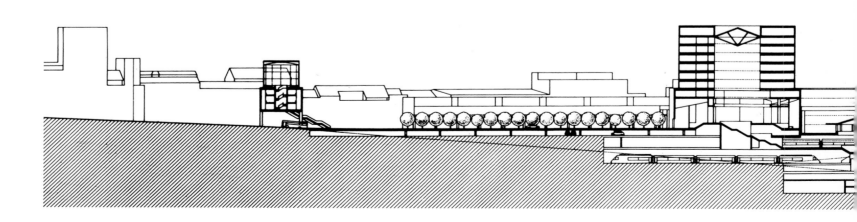

94

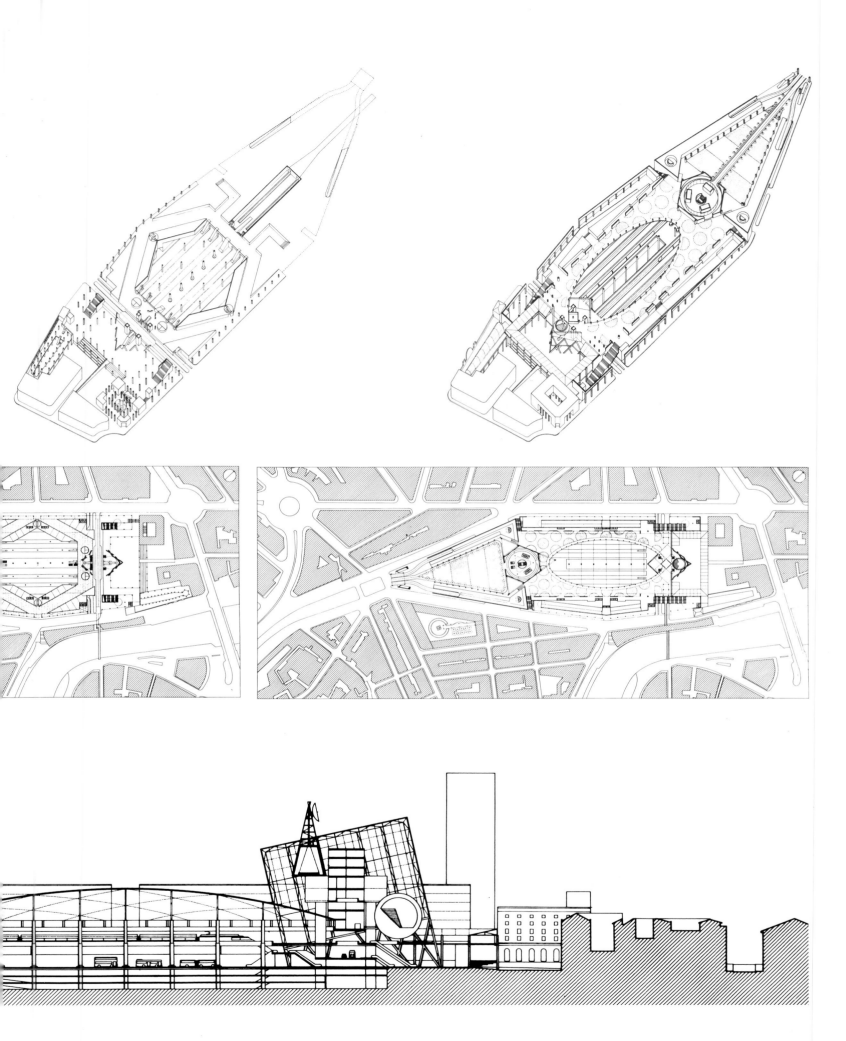

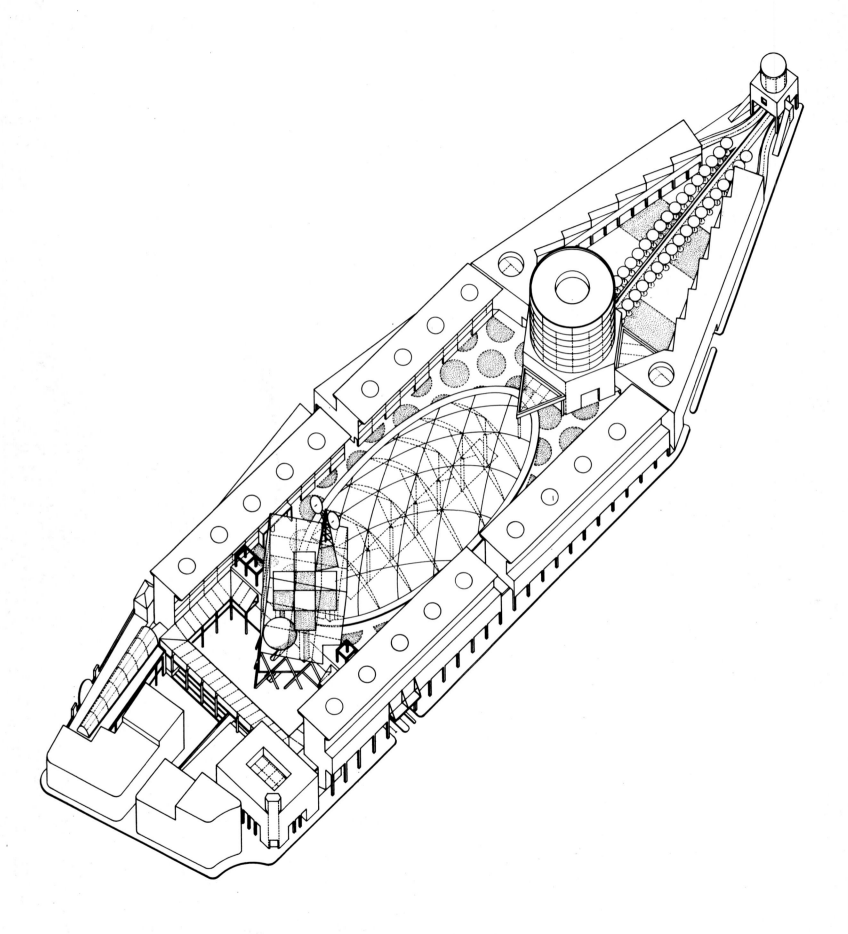

Axonometric

96